ENGLISH DRAMATISTS

Series Editor:
Bruce King

BAS

ENGLISH DRAMATISTS
Series Editor: Bruce King

Published titles

Susan Bassnett, *Shakespeare: The Elizabethan Plays*
Richard Cave, *Ben Jonson*
Christine Richardson and Jackie Johnston, *Medieval Drama*
Roger Sales, *Christopher Marlowe*
David Thomas, *William Congreve*
Martin White, *Middleton and Tourneur*
Katharine Worth, *Sheridan and Goldsmith*

Forthcoming titles

John Bull, *Vanbrugh and Farquhar*
Barbara Kachur, *Etheridge and Wycherley*
Philip McGuire, *Shakespeare: The Jacobean Plays*
Kate McLuskie, *Dekker and Heywood*
Maximillian Novak, *Fielding and Gay*
Rowland Wymer, *Webster and Ford*

ENGLISH DRAMATISTS

SHAKESPEARE
THE ELIZABETHAN PLAYS

Susan Bassnett

Professor at the Centre for British and Comparative Cultural Studies,
University of Warwick

150th YEAR

M

MACMILLAN

First published 1993 by
THE MACMILLAN PRESS LTD
Houndmills, Basingstoke, Hampshire RG21 2XS
and London
Companies and representatives
throughout the world

A catalogue record for this book is available
from the British Library.

ISBN 0–333–43782–9 hardcover
ISBN 0–333–43850–7 paperback

Typeset by Nick Allen/Longworth Editorial Services
Longworth, Oxon.

Printed in Hong Kong

Contents

Editor's Preface

Each generation needs to be introduced to the culture and great works of the past and to reinterpret them in its own ways. This series re-examines the important English dramatists of earlier centuries in the light of new information, new interests and new attitudes. The books are written for students, theatre-goers and general readers who want an up-to-date view of the plays and dramatists, with emphasis on drama as theatre and on stage, social and political history. Attention is given to what is known about performance, acting styles, changing interpretations, the stages and theatres of the time and theatre economics. The books will be relevant to those interested in or studying literature, theatre and cultural history.

BRUCE KING

Acknowledgements

A great many people have contributed to the writing of this book. I am particularly grateful to Clive Barker, the late Alois Bejblík, John Drakakis, Jirí Josek, Gunther Klotz, Agostino Lombardo, Philip McGuire, Martin Procházka, Zdenek Stríbrny and a host of other eminent Shakespeareans with whom many happy hours have been spent and who have taught me a great deal. Bruce King has been both a friend and editor, and my debt to him is immense. Thanks are due to Cathryn Tanner at Macmillan, and to Nick Allen in the final stages of editing. The manuscript was typed with her customary excellence by Irene Renshaw.

As always, I am indebted to those people in my domestic life that give me the space in which to write: my mother, Eileen Bassnett, my daughters Lucy, Vanessa and Rosie, the staff of the University of Warwick crèche, and Marlene Lawler.

Versions of Chapter 1 and Chapter 10 have appeared in the *Shakespeare Jahrbuch* (1984 and 1988).

Introduction

A fellowship in a cry of players
Hamlet

In a thought-provoking essay that examines how Brecht adapted Shakespeare, Margot Heinemann quotes an interview with the then Chancellor of the Exchequer, Nigel Lawson, in 1983, who claimed that Shakespeare must have been a good Tory.[1] That a British Conservative minister and a German Marxist playwright could each claim Shakespeare as their own is evidence of the way in which generations of readers constantly try to remake his work in their own image, and is also evidence of the very different traditions of reading Shakespeare that lie behind these apparently contradictory viewpoints. To understand this disparity, we should ignore the traditional claims for the 'universal significance' of Shakespeare's thought (the ploy of 'universality' has so often been used to disguise the real, deep-rooted issues that lie beneath the surface) and look instead at the history of responses to Shakespeare, at the way in which the image of Shakespeare grew and took shape in differing social and historical contexts.

In 1612, Elizabeth Weston, the Anglo-Latin poet hailed as the Tenth Muse died and was buried in Prague. Illustrious Humanists throughout Europe who had never heard of Shakespeare,

mourned her passing and wrote obituary poems to her.[2] Four
years later, in 1616, William Shakespeare died and was buried in
Stratford-upon-Avon. His remains were laid underneath the
floor of the chancel rather than outside in the churchyard, a sign
of his social status, at least to the inhabitants of the small
Warwickshire town in which he had been born and to which he
had retired, but his death went almost unremarked by the
outside world. By 1745, when the last edition of Elizabeth's
Weston's poems ever to be published appeared in Leipzig, she
was already fading from the public memory. Shakespeare, on the
contrary, was rising from the grave, and in 1769 a Jubilee celebration was held at Stratford, with the great Shakespearian actor
David Garrick delivering the Jubilee Oration. Shakespeare was
already well on his way to becoming the literary giant he had
never been during his lifetime and to achieving a fame that
would eventually eclipse Homer and Virgil, as classical studies
declined and English studies grew in the twentieth century.

By the 1840s, Shakespeare was being hailed as representative
of all that was valuable and significant in English culture.
Shakespeare was becoming an instrument of hegemony, a com-
batant on the side of imperialism. Lord Macauley's famous 1835
'Minute on Indian Education' states that one of the high points
of world cultural history was the Renaissance, and in asserting
the superiority of Western literature he goes so far as to suggest
that 'a single shelf of a good European library' is worth 'the
whole native literature of India and Arabia'.[3]

The image of Shakespeare as the epitome of all things English,
as England personified has continued to the present day. The
shaping of that image is a process connected to the version of
history that sees the Elizabethan age as one of England's greatest,
and looks back with nostalgia on a lost golden era. The rise of
film as a medium has added to this process by giving us a series
of visual images of the Elizabethan court, of Great Queen Bess
with her noble explorers Drake and Hawkins, her staunch
advisors, and Will, her chief poet and playwright. That Hawkins
started the iniquitous slave trade, that her advisors created one
of the most effective secret police systems in Europe, that
Shakespeare was, in Elizabeth's eyes, a slightly more subversive
than usual hack writer and that the queen herself accorded bear-
baiting higher status than the theatre for most of her life can be

conveniently ignored. Just as seventeenth-century Protestant historians created the myth of the Great Gloriana, so that myth came to be revised and enlarged in the Victorian age of imperialism and continues to prosper in the age of Elizabeth II. But there is an alternative version, both of Elizabeth's reign and of Shakespeare's greatness. In his essay of 1906 on Shakespeare, Tolstoy goes straight to the point, stating that Shakespeare's subsequent reputation owed more to the Germans (to Lessing, Goethe, Tieck and Schlegel) than to his fellow Englishmen:

> Until the end of the eighteenth century, Shakespeare not only failed to gain any special fame in England, but was valued less than his contemporary dramatists: Ben Jonson, Fletcher, Beaumont and others. His fame originated in Germany, and thence was transferred to England.[4]

Earlier, in 1839, Heinrich Heine had said that 'the Germans have comprehended Shakespeare better than the English'.[5] For the Germans did not discover in Shakespeare an archetypal Englishman; they discovered instead a revolutionary writer, whose works offered an opportunity to break the stranglehold of French classical theatre and who could provide German writers with a new model of tragedy. Significantly, a large number of Shakespeare's plays were translated into German, Italian, Polish, Hungarian, Czech and other languages of those European peoples engaged in a struggle to assert their national identity in the late eighteenth and early nineteenth centuries. This European Shakespeare was a writer who dared to challenge the Aristotelian unities, who created a new kind of powerful theatre in which ghosts walked, and Moors murdered innocent wives, and whose *Hamlet*, *Macbeth* and *King Lear* stood, according to Tieck, 'on the most extreme limits of the possible'.[6] Moreover, a dominant theme in Shakespeare, in the histories, comedies and tragedies, is the challenge to authority. Throughout his works, individuals confront tyranny and seek to topple or expose the usurper: Macduff finally destroys the tyrannous Macbeth; Rosalind's father returns from his exile in the Forest of Arden; Shylock does not get his pound of flesh; Richard II is overthrown, while Henry VI, the grandson of Henry IV who over-threw Richard, in turn, loses his own throne; Brutus joins in the assassination of Caesar but is ultimately defeated by the opportunistic Antony. There is an underlying thematic link between all these plays, and in the revolutionary ferment of early nineteenth-century Europe that theme had powerful appeal. It was also possible, in an age when theatre was heavily censored, to present an apparently innocuous classical English tragedy and then to argue that any subversive message was purely in the minds of the audience. If suspicious censors drew parallels between Austrian rulers and Macbeth or Claudius, then this could be argued away as being purely accidental. In such a climate it is easy to see how Shakespeare came to occupy such a prominent position in other literary systems, and why he should have become so well known to generations of readers and theatre-goers who may not even understand a word of the English language.

The gap between what can loosely be termed the English versions of Shakespeare and the European versions has never closed. What matters in the English versions is always, prin-cipally, the text. Schoolchildren are given the plays to read and told that the language marks the high point of English culture; critics continually attack any director who dares to tamper with the text; attempts at modernisation are still regarded with hos-tility, despite the fact that much of any Shakespearean play is obscure for contemporary audiences. Indeed, because of the difficulty many people experience with Shakespeare's language, performances in English all too often try far too hard to com-pensate with sets, costumes, stage business, and other devices. In languages other than English, however, Shakespearean produc-tions are very different indeed.

Freed from the constraints of the text, from having to speak every word of a classic text at all costs or be pilloried for desecra-tion of a sacred play, non-English speaking actors and directors can continue the tradition of experimentation. In translation, the language of Shakespeare's plays is unleashed, it is decanonised and the inherent energy can be released. Grigori Kozintsev, the Russian director whose film of *Hamlet* is a masterpiece of Shakespearean cinema, remarks that sometimes Shakespeare in his native tongue means very little:

The now academic English method of reading the full text in a rapid rhythm leads to a blunting of perception. In this flow of verse, the thoughts and images are not grasped, do not 'penetrate'. It is quite possible to speak all the words and to say little.[7]

So it is that translating Shakespeare has become an art in its own right, and that directors who tackle one of the plays in translation are able to say a great deal, often in radical ways unknown to their English counterparts. As Shakespeare has become more commercialised in the latter part of the twentieth century in Britain, so ironically have productions of the plays in English become less exciting and less innovative.[8] Since Peter Brook in the late 1960s, there has not been any English Shakespeare director of comparable status, but exciting productions of Shakespeare's plays have been staged in German, Italian, Swedish, Czech, Russian, Polish and Japanese, to name but a few. Outside the main theatres, small companies such as Footsbarn or Shared Experience have dared to desecrate the sacred texts, with positive results. Nevertheless the fact remains that a radical, revolutionary Shakespeare is a product of non-British consciousnesses and is not altogether acceptable to English minds, brought up in the tradition of Shakespeare's Englishness and taught to revere the majesty of his poetry even though they may not understand what he actually says. The great French actor, director and *homme de théâtre*, Jean-Louis Barrault argues that the English 'try with all their might' to hold Shakespeare back and 'to prevent him from crossing the water', while the French, like the rest of Europe, try to draw him to them.[9] He defends this statement by suggesting that Shakespeare is closer to the twentieth century than Molière, because the turmoil of Shakespeare's age mirrors the turmoil of our own. Quoting from *Henry VI, Part III*, the passage where the son who has killed his own father cries out 'O, pity, God, this miserable age!', Barrault says:

To us, who still have present in our minds the memory of Buchenwald and Auschwitz, the retreat of Dunkirk or the horrors endured by Coventry and Hiroshima, these cries of despair easily find an echo in our souls. . . . Shakespeare's age is, like ours, an age most aptly described by Hamlet's phrase 'The time is out of joint'.

To this list of horrors, from 1948 we could add the savage wars in Vietnam and Cambodia in the 1960s, the thousands of people who disappeared and were tortured to death throughout Latin America in the 1970s, the millions of famine victims, the unseen cloud of poison from Chernobyl of the 1980s, the Gulf War of 1991 and the contrast that grows ever wider between the consumerism of the industrialised world and the starvation of the rest in the 1990s.

Shakespeare's own world was far from the golden age of Good Queen Bess, mythologised and packaged for tourists in shops at Stratford-upon-Avon. The latter years of Elizabeth I's reign were fraught with problems. Having inherited a poverty-stricken country with hostile neighbours, Elizabeth and her government struggled to keep the country from bankruptcy. An early success was to make peace with the Scots, and when Shakespeare was a child of five in 1569, the Northern Rising was successfully thwarted. Despite the crisis of the mid-1570s in the Low Countries, England refrained from military intervention, but in 1585 Elizabeth had to send in English troops. Corruption in the army (a favourite Shakespearean motif in the history plays) was rife, and while starving soldiers begged in the streets, their captains and commanders made huge profits at the queen's expense – at one stage in the Low Countries campaign the Earl of Leicester knighted fourteen captains in one day, while in the Irish campaign his stepson, the Earl of Essex ennobled his own corrupt supporters. The defeat of the Spanish Armada in 1588 was hailed as a triumph for England in that it effectively put an end to fears of invasion by the Spaniards, but it cost the country dearly in economic terms, as did the Irish campaigns of 1598–1601. Foreign policy was not the only cause of the economic crisis; the enclosure of common lands and the spread of monopolies altered the earlier pattern of social hierarchies. A new land-hungry gentry was being created, while property speculators were everywhere. The Act for the Punishment of Vagabonds of 1572 ensured that those who had been made homeless by the shifting economic changes were punished still further by being whipped or branded if they attempted to beg for a crust of bread. Far from being a world of cosy thatched cottages where stout yeomen and their families expressed warm sentiments of national pride and affection for their sovereign, the last decades of Elizabeth's reign provide a picture of a country riven by economic crises and religious dissent, where plague periodically swept through the land (plague closed the theatres with alarming frequency, as in 1581–2, 1592–3, 1603–4), where profiteering was rife and where the innocent were often made homeless and turned out to die of starvation or disease. The rottenness of the state of Denmark reflected the rottenness of Shakespeare's homeland, and the paranoia of the Danish court served as a reminder of the paranoia of the last years of Elizabeth's reign, when Essex raised his abortive rebellion and died on the block in 1601. (*Hamlet*, of course, was written around the same time, at the height of the Irish crisis, probably in late 1600 to early 1601, though there is some controversy as to the exact date.)

Of Shakespeare's own life we know surprisingly little, a situation that has provided material for endless speculation. The eighteenth-century editor George Steevens (*sic*) commented succinctly that:

> All that is known with any degree of certainty concerning Shakespeare, is: that he was born in Stratford-upon-Avon; married and had children there; went to London, where he commenced actor, and wrote poems and plays; returned to Stratford, made his will, died, and was buried.[10]

This brief statement more or less sums up the bare bones of Shakespeare's biography, though more flesh can be added when we look at the evidence of the texts he left behind, not only his thirty-seven plays, long narrative poems and sonnets, but also legal documents, the first of which is the entry in the parish register of Holy Trinity church in Stratford recording the baptism of William, son of John Shakespeare and Mary Arden on 26 April 1564. We cannot even be sure of his date of birth, though his birthday is celebrated on 23 April, coincidentally the feast day of the patron saint of England, St George. S. Schoenbaum's huge, highly enjoyable book on the history of Shakespearian biography shows some of the intricate solutions devised by biographers to explain some of the absences or anomalies in the traces of Shakespeare's life left behind for our scrutiny. For example, the fact that he owned property in his native town has been seized upon to indicate his aspirations to gentility and used to argue that he was an innate conservative, whilst the fact that he left his wife his 'second-best bed' in his will has often been taken to indicate a breakdown in the marriage. Schoenbaum notes this interpretation, along with a counterview that the bed may have had sentimental associations and that Shakespeare may have intended the bequest as a demonstration of affection, rather than neglect. He also adds the point that according to English law a widow was entitled to one third of her husband's goods in any case, and so there was no need to state that fact in a will.[11] This particular story is a good example of the endlessly varied speculation about Shakespeare the Man, culled from all kinds of disparate sources.

Virginia Woolf invented the biography of an imaginary sister, to demonstrate the kind of constraints under which women were compelled to live in contrast to the freedom of movement enjoyed by a young aspiring actor-playwright in the last years of the sixteenth century. There is even a suggestion that Shakespeare's younger brother, Edmund, may also have been an actor. Only one of Shakespeare's actual sisters outlived him, the others dying in infancy or childhood. Certainly we know that Shakespeare's wife apparently remained in Stratford, and his children were born and baptised there – Susanna in 1583 and twins, Hamnet and Judith, in 1585. Although both daughters survived their father, Hamnet died in 1596 at the age of eleven. Again, it is purely speculation, but both *King John* and *The Merchant of Venice*, which were probably written in 1596, contain the motif of the lost child – Constance mourns her murdered son Arthur, Shylock grieves for his lost daughter, Jessica; and in the two parts of *Henry IV*, which probably date from 1597–8, a central theme is the problematic relationship between fathers and sons, with Henry IV and Falstaff as father-figures, and Prince Henry and Harry Hotspur as contrasting sons. Scores of critics have pointed to the similarity between the name Hamnet and the tormented son of Shakespeare's imagination, Hamlet, Prince of Denmark.

Nothing can be proven one way or another. Already before the death of his son, family relationships had been foregrounded in

Shakespeare's writing. In *Henry VI, Part 3* there is the moving scene where father kills son and son kills father unknowingly in the bloodiness of civil war, in *Titus Andronicus* even the monstrous Aaron and Tamara have feelings for their children, *Romeo and Juliet* shows the conflict between generations turning into tragedy, while *A Midsummer Night's Dream* shows how that same conflict can exist but be miraculously resolved. Hermia's father is prepared for his daughter either to enter a convent or be put to death if she continues to refuse the husband he has chosen for her, but by the end of the play all is happily settled. Throughout his plays, Shakespeare deals with the various ways in which parents and children suffer, sometimes because they inflict pain upon each other, as with Lear and his daughters, or Leontes and Perdita, or because they are vulnerable to attack because of their love for each other, as with Macduff whose family is brutally murdered by Macbeth's henchmen. We can take this recurrent theme in several ways – as evidence of Shakespeare's love for his own children and grief at the death of his son; as evidence of the way in which the family could be symbolically used as a microcosm of the state and of social order, with the parent at its head and children committed to obedience, like subjects before their monarch; as evidence of Shakespeare's stagecraft, showing how he recognised that the depiction of filial ingratitude will heighten the temperature of an audience, while the murder of children shown on stage will cause shock and outrage through its fusion of theatricality and realism. Possibly all these explanations can be conflated; certainly we cannot deduce anything decisive.

If we cannot be certain of very much about Shakespeare's life, we cannot either be very sure about the facts concerning his plays. Of course we have the texts that have come down to us in various editions as the Works of Shakespeare, but the debates on the dating, staging and possible co-authoring of texts have been fiercely fought, and are likely to continue. In 1986 the Oxford Edition of the *Complete Works*, edited by Stanley Wells and Gary Taylor, included *The Two Noble Kinsmen* and *All is True* (*Henry VIII*) in addition to the accepted canon of plays, and aroused a great deal of critical hostility as a result.

Shakespeare is such a canonical author, with the plays staged throughout the world and read by each new generation, that it is often hard to remind ourselves that the apparent rigidity this status conveys on the texts is a recent invention, for in their day, the plays themselves were treated very differently. M. M. Reese reminds us that when Ben Jonson collected his plays together and revised and edited them under the title of his Works, this was regarded as both pretentious and silly.[12] Reese points out that plays were regarded as ephemeral things and argues that the practice of making plays bears this out:

> Often a play would be commissioned by the actors only a few weeks before it would be needed on the stage. The first stage in its creation would be a tavern conference between the company's representatives and one or more playwrights . . . in extreme cases as many as five writers contributed to a single play . . . we have no means of knowing how often Shakespeare may have been called upon to 'dress' an imperfect piece written for his company. Collaboration was not welcomed by the playwrights because it meant a splitting of the fee . . . it was in such circumstances that Chettle had a hand in forty-eight plays for Henslowe within a period of five years, and Heywood reckoned that in a long career he had 'either an entire hand or at the least a main finger' in 220 plays. That collaboration could have flourished to such an extent was partly a consequence of the general assumption that the play was a perishable thing.[13]

Financial considerations, as always in theatre, weighed as heavily as artistic ones, if not more so. Those readers who fondly imagine Shakespeare quietly writing at a desk with his quill pen and then arriving at the theatre with the finished script for a company of enthusiastic, disciplined actors are misled by romantic novelists or Hollywood film-makers. The reality was very different. Despite having some small security by being part of a licensed company, performers lived precariously, and from the information on the income of Shakespeare's company at the Rose in 1592–3 they were by no means well paid. Plague could and did close the theatres, companies were forced to tour in the absence of sufficient theatre spaces in which to play regularly, and competition was strong. A better picture of the working life of Shakespeare and his fellow players is that of the lifestyle in

our own times of some Alternative Theatre or Third Theatre
companies working today – compelled to keep touring, working
with small budgets, devising performances at great speed and
making constant changes to the shows as they perform.
Companies were small, and actors played several roles in each
show, developing stock roles that changed according to age and
development of skills. The Players in *Hamlet* provide some
insight into the company structure. When Hamlet greets the
Players in II. 2, he remarks on the way the actors have aged –
one has grown a beard, another is on the verge of growing out
of female parts:

Welcome good friends – Oh, my old friend! Thy face is
valanced since I saw thee last. Coms't thou to beard me in
Denmark? – What, my young lady and mistress? By'r Lady,
your ladyship is nearer heaven than when I saw you last by
the altitude of a chopine. Pray God your voice, like a piece of
uncurrent gold, be not cracked within the ring.

And in the same scene Polonius announces that the actors are
infinitely versatile:

The best actors in the world, either for tragedy, comedy,
history, pastoral, pastoral-comical, historical-pastoral, tragi-
cal-historical, tragical-comical-historical-pastoral, scene indivi-
dable or poem unlimited. Seneca cannot be too heavy, nor
Plautus too light. For the law of writ and the liberty, these are
the only men.

As an actor grew older, so he would move from one type of
role to another, and the chronological development of Shakespeare's plays is also a history of changes in the company. It
seems very likely that the original company consisted of strong
comedians, and studies of Shakespeare's clowns show the
changes in style as actors moved on. The slapstick foolery of the
earlier comedies changes into a more laconic style, with the fool-
ing becoming more satirical and bitter. The clowning of *The
Comedy of Errors* or *The Taming of the Shrew* is in a different style
altogether than than of *Twelfth Night* or *As You Like It*.
It has been suggested that this change in comic playing, along

with the popularity of the braggart figure, the *miles gloriosus*, is indicative of an increasing move towards tragedy, especially after the great clown William Kemp left the company in 1599. Baldwin, a pioneering 'theatre studies' Shakespearian critic, suggests that the 'natural inclination' of younger members of the company was towards tragedy, and that once Kemp had gone, Shakespeare wrote increasingly for the different talents his company possessed.[14] This may well be the case, but it is also likely that after the Act of 1572 there were very strong divisions of performance skills. The Act for the Punishment of Vagabonds, as it was termed, distinguished between performers in the pay of a Baron of the realm or 'any other honorable personage of greater degree' and performers defined variously as 'Juglers, Pedlars, Mynstrels, Comon Players in Enterludes, Bearwards etc.' who might now be arrested and 'deemd Roges Vacaboundes and Sturdy Beggers'. I have suggested elsewhere that the implications of this Act for theatre have yet to be fully understood, and that one aspect of this change may well have meant the relegation of female performers to alternative, unlicensed companies, thus propagating the myth that there had never been any women players in England until the Restoration, despite all the evidence to the contrary.[15]

Certainly Shakespeare's performers were all male, but by the time of his first plays (at least, so far as we know they were his first) the Act had been in force almost twenty years and the commercial theatre in England had developed very rapidly, not least in the way in which plays were being produced and marketed. What does seem clear, however, is that from 1572 the companies under patronage placed an increasing importance on the play, thus highlighting the division between a text-based theatre and alternative forms. It seems reasonable to assume, therefore, that players trained prior to 1572 may well have had various skills, including, for example, acrobatic and musical skills that were less necessary in more structured plays and in specially built theatres. This same distinction prevails today, if we look at the kind of skills required by a performer in the Odin Teatret, or in Footsbarn and those required by actors in the Royal Shakespeare Company. Likewise, a generation of clowns who were not trained in music hall or in vaudeville, such as have appeared at the end of the twentieth century, are very different from the clowns of thirty or forty years earlier. Something similar must have happened in the latter years of the sixteenth century, which is not to say that there was not an ongoing popular comic tradition, but simply to point out that the training of actors changed, which in turn changed the kind of material those actors needed as the basis of their work.

Chambers quotes Edmond Howes's version of that change, which offers a completely different picture:

> Comedians and stage-players of former time were very poor and ignorant in respect of these of this time: but being now grown very skilful and exquisite actors for all matters, they were entertained into the service of divers great lords: out of which companies there were twelve of the best chosen, and, at the request of Sir Francis Walsingham, they were sworn the queens servants and were allowed wages and liveries as grooms of the chamber: and until this yeare 1583, the queene had no players.[16]

Howes's argument is all too well known in any age: he suggests that standards rose with the advent of patronage. The actors, he says, are far more skilful than those of former times, and evidence of their skill is their preferment in noble circles. Yet as anyone with any practical knowledge of theatre will recognise, there is a whole absent text in Howes's picture of the improvement of artistic standards. We can only imagine how actors must have scrambled for that preferment, for the chance to wear a uniform and be paid a regular wage, and we can only speculate on what kind of performance skills were lost, deemed less exquisite for courtly tastes, where linguistic games prevailed over physical technique. The queen, it should be noted, is indicative of the way in which current taste regarding theatre changed; her earlier preference for music, dancing and bear-baiting kept her without a company of players until 1583, but thereafter the importance of players in court circles would continue to grow. The division between 'high' theatre with its roots in the text and 'low' theatre continued until well into the twentieth century, and to some extent is still with us today.

Reading Shakespeare, on the page and on the stage, at the end of the twentieth century cannot help but reflect the changes that are taking place at the present time. Since the 1960s, literary criticism has been in turmoil, with a plethora of methodologies and reading strategies that have appeared (and sometimes disappeared again) with bewildering speed. Theatre Studies has developed as a serious academic discipline, finding its way into schools and universities, so the old divide between theatre practice and book-based academic study seems to be a little less rigid. Particularly useful to readers today is the work done on the Elizabethan and Jacobean theatre, from the point of view of playing spaces, finances, company structure, acting methods, audience composition and so forth, so that we now know that whilst Shakespeare was skilled in his use of metaphorical language, he was also considering which actors he had to hand, and what had been successful last time with an audience, as well as how much room the actors had to get on and off stage at speed. Practical considerations were significant, and that is something that a great deal of literary criticism, which has focused on the language of the characters, has disregarded. Moreover, the New Historicist approach has opened up ways of looking at the plays as products of a particular moment in time, reflecting the ambiguities and the prejudices of the topical issues of the day. At the same time, notions of plural reading strategies have removed the fear that once haunted readers, the fear that they may somehow be reading wrongly. Pluralism in reading simply means that the reader takes a new responsibility in the act of reading, instead of trying to sift through a text for some unknown piece of received wisdom or absolute truth.

Approaches to Shakespeare today are richly varied. We have learned to discard the worst of formalist excesses in literary criticism, whilst at the same time learning a lot about how a text works by understanding the processes of formalist analysis; we have the new scholarship in theatre history to draw upon, and we know enough about the variations of interpretation of Shakespeare over the centuries to recognise that there is no ultimate, final, definitive reading of any text, though obviously there are historical constraints that need to be regarded. So, for example, although a twentieth-century reader is likely to note anti-Semitism in *The Merchant of Venice*, Shakespeare, as a product of his own age, would have been familiar with the kind of black anti-Semitic comedy represented by Marlowe's *Jew of*

Malta, for example, and his audience would have enjoyed seeing a stereotyped figure of contempt appear on the stage, and ultimately be the loser. Yet a Western reader today cannot approach anti-Semitism without a sense of outrage, because after the Holocaust it is not possible to see Jews as stage figures of fun or derision. So some directors and critics have sought to impose their own twentieth-century ethical view onto Shakespeare, who, as a man of the Renaissance, was simply working with stereotypes that were acceptable in his own time. For us as readers, to deal with that apparent contradiction, we need to recognise the dialectics of a reading that takes into account both the ordinariness of anti-Semitisim in the sixteenth century and the abomination of anti-Semitism today. These two opposites do not cancel each other out; they coexist in a relationship that cannot be ignored.

Since we have so few certainties about Shakespeare, and since editors, critics, directors and actors have made and remade him so many times, speculations about his life and work will not disappear. Indeed, this present book is in its way another tentative approach: I am suggesting that the best way to approach Shakespeare today, given the methodologies of criticism and analysis that we have at our disposal, is to see him not so much as a *great universal figure* but rather as a canny, practical writer, someone whose skill and knowledge of theatre resulted in the creation of some of the most memorable plays ever to be devised in any culture, at any time. The world in which he lived was a troubled one; his theatre was a precarious, marginalised activity in a constant state of flux; we know little of his life, except that by the end he desired security and managed to acquire it to some small degree, retiring to his native town and living in what must have been reasonable comfort. What he was not was what he has become: a monolithic figure whose texts have been taken as holy writ and interpreted by generations of wise men and women. The image of Shakespeare given to schools is all too often as a dull pedant, and the fact that he is presented as the high priest of English culture does not help at all. Students are rarely told that plays are often the result of collaborations between actors and writers, and the general idea of theatre is still one where playwrights produce finished versions for actors to rehearse inside theatres, rather than the kind of theatre-making produced by truly great contemporaries of ours such as Peter Brook, Jerzy Grotowski and Eugenio Barba.

If, in this last decade of the twentieth century, the ghost of Shakespeare were to return to us, four hundred years after the first production of his plays, he would no doubt be amazed by the story of the glorification of his own image, a story that far exceeds anything of his own imagining. From his origins as an actor-writer in Elizabethan England he has passed into mythology, becoming a household name not only in his own country but throughout the world. He has influenced an uncountable number of other writers, his plays have delighted audiences in countries that did not even exist when they were first staged. Generations of critics have analysed every word he ever wrote, first by candlelight and then by computer. He ranks with Homer as one of the all-time greats, and has even overtaken Homer, as knowledge of Greek declines rapidly, and fewer and fewer readers ever encounter the *Iliad* or the *Odyssey*, even in translation.

Whole schools of Shakespearean scholarship have arisen; critical trends pass like waves, each leaving its trace on the shoreline. Production techniques have varied radically over the centuries, the plays have been revised and rewritten, staged with casts of hundreds and gigantic budgets or performed minimally, by single actors in bare rooms. There are operas based on the plays, plays based on the plays, novels based on the plays, all created in an unending process of reflection and refraction. We know as little as we ever did of Shakespeare's life, but the works remain our inheritance.

Like many people, I remember very clearly my first encounter with Shakespeare. I was seven years old, and I went to see *As You Like It*, in a production staged by my mother in the gardens of the British Embassy in Lisbon. I can remember details of that night that have stayed with me, despite all the later versions of the play that I have seen since. I remember sitting up high on a scaffolding, with a fountain beneath me and feeling that I, too, was in the Forest of Arden. I had no way of judging the artistic quality of the production, the standard of acting, the success or failure of the evening. It was simply, essentially, wonderful and looking back, I realise that on that night I first experienced theatre as magical. Despite all the years I have spent studying Shakespeare, performing in his plays, teaching his works and now, writing this book, the memory of that one magical night is the greatest tribute I feel I can pay to the man who was a master of his craft.

1
Sexuality and Power in the Three Parts of *King Henry VI*

A great deal of critical attention has been paid to the way in which Shakespeare explored contemporary structuring of power relationships in his plays. Stephen Greenblatt has argued that Shakespeare's plays are 'centrally and repeatedly concerned with the production and containment of subversion and disorder'.[1] Furthermore, he suggests that notions of Elizabethan power are:

> inseparably bound up with the figure of Queen Elizabeth, a ruler without a standing army, without a highly developed bureaucracy, without an extensive police force, a ruler whose power is constituted in theatrical celebrations of royal glory and theatrical violence visited upon the enemies of that glory. . . . Elizabethan power . . . depends upon its privileged visibility.[2]

The development of complex state apparatuses in the centuries following the death of Elizabeth was paralleled by the increasing invisibility of the forces of authority. Similarly, the increasing marginalisation of the feminine was accompanied by the steady disappearance of women from positions of public power. It is not too far-fetched to trace the beginnings of this process in Shakespeare's work, and to note that alongside the obvious focus on issues of subversion and disorder he also focused on the vexed question of public and private femininity.

During the Renaissance, attitudes to women changed. As the active (masculine) life came to be valued higher than the contemplative (feminine) life, so the status of the feminine, and of women in general, was altered. During the age of Humanism, vast numbers of women writers, painters, performers, intellectuals and patrons of the arts were to be found throughout Europe. Educational theorists pronounced not only on the education of princes, but also on the education of women, and court salons took up and developed the debate. In Spain, France, Italy and England, women ruled states, either in their own right or in lieu of a child or absent husband. And yet by the latter part of the seventeenth century, the beginning of the supposed Enlightenment, the public role of women had been dramatically reduced. In the age of Reason, the feminine came to represent unreason, the antithesis of all that was socially desirable, the wild darkness of nature's jungle.

The transition from accepting to denigrating femininity was already under way in the latter years of the reign of Elizabeth. Portraits of Elizabeth herself gradually shifted emphasis from portraying the private woman to showing images of a public ruler, a symbol of national greatness. Frances Yates and Roy Strong have demonstrated how iconographical portrayals of Elizabeth underwent various changes during her reign,[3] perhaps most clearly demonstrated in the portrayals of the queen after the defeat of the Spanish Armada in 1588. The 1592 portrait in the National Portrait Gallery shows her standing upon a map of the realm, dressed in an elaborate gown with a huge hooped skirt and great crested ruff round her neck. Whereas in many of the earlier portraits the emphasis is on a particular feature (her profile, hair, hands and so on) or as a symbol of chastity and virtue, the later portraits emphasise her garments. Representing femininity and power clearly had begun to cause problems; the answer lay in ritualised representations of superficial signs of femininity, whilst maintaining the image of (masculine) power. Elizabeth herself seems to have been all too aware of this ambiguity. In her famous speech to the army at Tilbury before the arrival of the Armada, she took pains to play off her female traits (inherited naturally) against her role as sovereign. On horseback, holding a truncheon in her hands, she reviewed the army and is reputed to have told them:

> I am come amongst you, as you see, at this time, not for my recreation and disport, but being resolved, in the midst and heat of the battle, to live or die amongst you all, to lay down for my God and for my kingdom, and for my people, my honour and my blood, even in the dust. I know I have the body of a weak and feeble woman, but I have the heart and stomach of a king, and of a king of England too.[4]

The political power she held as ruler had to be asserted against her sex and, simultaneously, her femininity could be used as an instrument in winning over the loyalty of her men. It is a strategy that has continually been employed by the few women who have attained positions of similar power to Elizabeth in ensuing centuries.

Although the cult of Elizabeth worship developed during her reign, this did not by any means signify a more positive attitude to women in society in general. Misogynist pamphlets increased in number and virulence from the 1580s onwards, and educational theorists began to argue for the inability of women to study certain subjects. It is particularly interesting to note that whilst many Renaissance woman, amongst whom Elizabeth I herself, were praised especially for their skills in language learning and their ability to discourse in Latin, the study of languages amongst women appears to have been one of the first areas to be declared unfeminine. By the end of the seventeenth century, women who studied Latin, and the tiny minority with any Greek, were regarded as unusual, often looked upon disparagingly as unfemininely intellectual. In wider social terms, the status of women further deteriorated with a hardening of marital property laws, the decision of the Church of England to prohibit divorce in 1604, the steady elimination of women from areas of skilled labour. The process begun in the latter part of the sixteenth century was the marginalisation of women in public life and the invention of an idea of femininity based on domesticity and seclusion – a process that was only to be checked two centuries later with the empassioned pleading of

Mary Wollstonecroft and the new breed of revolutionary feminists.

In the twentieth century, feminist criticism of Shakespeare has examined the whole question of sexuality in his plays, though attention has tended to be trained on the problem plays, the later comedies and on the tragedies. The histories on the whole have largely been considered as a series of plays dealing primarily with problems of succession and revolution, plays which, as their titles suggest, are about kings and king-making rather than sexual relations.

Most neglected of all the histories by all critics regardless of sex have tended to be the three parts of *Henry VI*. Yet this attitude in no way reflects the success of those same plays in their own time. As Andrew Cairncross points out in his introduction to the Arden edition of *The Third Part of Henry VI*, the plays, together with *Richard III*, were extremely popular when they first appeared:

> Thomas Nashe the dramatist bore witness to the 'ten thousand spectators at the least' who, 'at several times,' saw brave Talbot (in *1 Henry VI*) bleeding on the boards of the Theatre. When the dying Robert Greene looked round for a shaft to throw at his too successful rival, he found the line (not yet in print) of *3 Henry VI*, which he knew well enough to parody – 'his tiger's heart wrapped in a player's (woman's) hide'. The first of Shakespeare's plays to be printed after *Titus Andronicus*, were *2* and *3 Henry VI*, in pirated versions (1594, 1595) and *Richard III* followed not long after (1597). These versions of *2* and *3 Henry VI* were each twice reprinted before the Folio of 1623, that of *Richard III* five times. The quality of the reports, moreover, especially those of *3 Henry VI* and *Richard III*, was high. All these facts confirm the popularity of the series.[5]

The three parts of *Henry VI* cover the period from 1430 to 1471, with considerable juggling of historical time to accommodate the requirements of plot and dramatic structure. So, for example, although Joan of Arc was burned in 1431, in *Henry VI, Part 1* Joan la Pucelle, as she is known, fights in a battle that took place in 1451, and in *Henry VI, Part 2* Eleanor Cobham is represented as a contemporary of Queen Margaret, despite the fact that her fall from favour had already taken place before the arrival of Margaret in the English court. That Shakespeare took liberties with the time sequences of historical events as recounted in the chronicles is well known; what concerns us here is the careful structuring of events in order to focus attention on specific incidents or characters, in particular female characters.

The debates on the chronology of writing the three parts of *Henry VI* are well known and too extensive to be repeated here. For present purposes, I have chosen to accept 1590 as a focal point, since all the evidence suggests that none of the plays pre-dates 1587, and *Henry VI, Part 2* (and most likely *Henry VI, Part 3*) do actually date from 1590, with *Henry VI, Part 1* probably having been written between that date and early 1592. In other words, the plays were written in the period immediately following the major crises of the Babington plot (1586), the execution of Mary Stuart (1587), the invasion of the Spanish Armada (1588) and Elizabeth's attempt to break the power of Puritan Parliamentary radicals (1587 to the early 1590s).

The structural order of the three parts of *Henry VI* is very linear: *Part 1* ends with Suffolk prophecying that:

> Margaret shall now be queen and rule the King
> But I will rule both her, the King, and realm.
> (V. viii. 107–8)

After the French wars in *Henry VI, Part 1*, attention shifts to the civil strife that will ensue, following the marriage of Henry VI to a French princess with no dowry and a sexual preference for another man. *Henry VI, Part 2* takes up this story, following the career of the Queen's lover, Suffolk to the moment of his assassination, and simultaneously follows the fall of Gloucester and his wife Eleanor, and the collapse of Jack Cade's rebellion. The play ends with Henry and Margaret fleeing before the advance of York's troops. Margaret is now firmly in charge of policy-making and berates Henry for his cowardice and indecision.

Henry VI, Part 3 opens with the Yorkist troops acknowledging that Henry's escape has been successful, and the play follows the acceleration of the civil war, culminating finally in the death of

Henry's son, the crowning of York's son as Edward IV and the murder of Henry by Edward's brother, Richard. Edward's concluding speech looks forward to a time of renewal and regeneration:

> And now what rests but that we spend the time
> With stately triumphs, mirthful comic shows,
> Such as befits the pleasure of the court?
> Sound drum and trumpets! Farewell, sour annoy!
> For here, I hope, begins our lasting joy.
>
> (V. vii. 41–5)

Edward's short-sightedness is treated ironically; any possibility of lasting joy has already been destroyed during the course of the play. His alienation of the French king through his rejection of the Lady Bona in favour of Elizabeth Woodville and the casual manner in which he ships off the deposed Margaret ('Away with her and waft her hence to France') has ensured him enemies overseas. At home, his preferment of his new wife's relatives has alienated many, including his own brothers, and the fourth play in the series, *Richard III*, opens with a monologue that deliberately mocks the hopeful tone of Edward's final speech. Good intentions and hopes of better happenings are not enough in a world torn apart by civil strife.

Whilst it is clear that these plays are concerned with political instability and attempts at subversion, all three use images of femininity as central metaphors in the delineation of events. *Henry VI, Part 1* focuses on maidens, on the two figures of Joan la Pucelle, virgin turned warrior, and the Countess of Auvergne, who tries to win a reputation for herself by taking Talbot prisoner. *Henry VI, Part 2* focuses on wives, on the unfaithful but politically cunning Margaret and the over-proud Eleanor who resorts to witchcraft to help her with her plans. Eleanor, the commoner, is crushed by the power of Margaret and the nobility, just as Jack Cade is destroyed by that same power, which wins over the hearts and minds of his rebel army through an appeal to national pride. Alone and starving, Cade is killed by Iden, the Kentish gentleman enjoying a quiet walk on his estate.

Henry VI, Part 3 presents two queens, Margaret, the avenging, militaristic French wife of a king unwilling to fight, and Elizabeth, the new breed of queen from the minor English aristocratic family, who wins over the affection of the king through her sexuality and whose role appears to be that of bedmate and mother to numerous children by her two husbands.

Common to all three plays are the differences between the female characters, differences that in *Henry VI, Part 2* emerge as open conflict between Margaret and Eleanor. Only in *Richard III* are differences between women less than the common suffering which binds them, and the female characters in this play bear witness both to the monstrous evil of Richard and the wretchedness of individuals when the nation is divided within itself and wrongly governed.

The maiden–wife–queen–mother images coincide with the maturing of Henry, whom we encounter in infancy and follow through to manhood and eventual deposition and death. But the female characters also have another function. In all three plays they are associated with attitudes, emotions and actions that are negatively judged. They provide examples of unwomanliness and unqueenliness, in short, they are presented to us as violating natural order in several different ways.

In *Henry VI, Part 1*, Joan la Pucelle first appears armed, in I. iii, and defeats Charles in single combat, thereby convincing him of the validity of her claims to be inspired by God. It is notable that Joan refers to the Virgin Mary, claiming she first appeared to her in a vision. To an Elizabethan audience, these references would serve as a powerful reminder of the presence of Catholicism, within the world of the play and in their own. While Joan conquers Charles, the nobles comment on their relationship in terms that closely parallel III. ii of *Henry VI, Part 3* when Richard and Clarence comment on the exchange between Elizabeth and Edward. Throughout the play, Charles refers to Joan in terms of reverence, even suggesting that she will be canonised and made the saint of France. In sharp contrast to this religiosity, Talbot talks of Joan in terms of witchcraft. She is 'railing Hecate' (III. vi), a creature who has overstepped the boundaries of womanhood by taking upon herself the role of a man. After Talbot's death, presented in terms that clearly show him to be the heroic examplar of the play, his doubts are proved true when Fiends appear to Joan and finally, she repudiates her own father and admits to fornication with several men in an attempt to save herself from the stake. The saintly figure suggested in the early part of the play is transformed into a squalid harriden, prophesying death and misery as she is led off to execution.

In counterpoint to Joan is the figure of the Countess of Auvergne. She attempts to capture Talbot using not military strength but feminine wiles. She fails because she has no insight; she completely misunderstands the appearance and reality of a hero, refusing to believe that Talbot is who he claims to be since she perceives him as a 'weak and writhled shrimp' (II. iii. 22). As soon as he proves his claim, by bringing in his soldiers, she reverses her position and offers him hospitality and flattery. She is the personification of inconstancy and deceit, a woman who acts out of desire for fame and glory, has no understanding or perception, and changes her mind as soon as she is put in a position of compromise. When the character of Margaret is introduced in V. v, we have become so accustomed to negative images of women that it seems hardly likely that she will be any different. Almost immediately she succumbs to Suffolk and the play ends with Henry agreeing to give away his French lands as bride-price.

The witchcraft is continued in *Henry VI, Part 2*. Eleanor Cobham consults with Margery Jourdain and other dubious figures in an attempt to discover the future. She dreams of power, of Henry and Margaret transformed into her subjects, and tries to tempt her husband, Gloucester with this ambition. Eleanor's downfall leaves the field clear for Margaret, who becomes a figure strongly reminiscent of Lady Macbeth, urging Suffolk and Henry to exert greater strength. When taking leave of Suffolk in III. ii, Margaret accuses him of unmanliness:

> Fie, coward woman and soft-hearted wretch!
> Hast thou not spirit to curse thine enemy?
>   (III. ii. 306–7)

After Suffolk's death the transformation of Margaret into avenger is complete; she appears in IV. iv, lamenting over Suffolk's head, saying that her hopes have been destroyed with him. From this point onwards she becomes the military leader of the Lancastrian cause. York refers to her as a 'blood-bespotted Neapolitan . . . England's bloody scourge' (V. i. 118–19).

In *Henry VI, Part 3* Margaret the vengeful warrior is aided by
her son, who rejects Henry's attempts at compromise. Berating
Henry for his cowardice, she contrasts his weakness with her
own strength:

> Had I been there, which am a silly woman,
> The soldiers should have toss'd me on their pikes
> Before I would have granted to that act;
> But thou prefer'st thy life before thine honour
>
> (I. i. 250–3)

Margaret's desire for revenge leads her to still greater excesses,
in particular the torture of York before his murder, which recalls
the scourging of Christ in the mystery plays, when she gives him
a cloth soaked in the blood of his own young son. York's agony,
and his fatherly love, contrast sharply with Margaret's ruth-
lessness. In one of the best-known speeches of the play, York
accuses Margaret of being less than a woman:

> O tiger's heart wrapp'd in a woman's hide!
> How coulds't thou drain the life-blood of the child,
> To bid the father wipe his eyes withal,
> And yet be seen to bear a woman's face?
> Woman are soft, mild, pitiful, and flexible;
> Thou stern, indurate, flinty, rough, remorseless.
>
> (I. iv. 137–42)

Margaret is not only an unnatural woman in that she fights
like a man, she is unnatural because she lacks those feelings that
women should have. The imagery of bestiality, together with
imagery of shipwreck and disaster runs through Margaret's own
language and the language of those around her, stressing her
destructive role. Only at the end of *Henry VI, Part 3*, when her
own son is murdered, does Margaret behave 'like a woman',
showing the strength of her maternal feelings in terms very close
to those of York in I. iv. By this point in the trilogy, the central
villain is now Richard, and Margaret's outbursts are directed
principally at him. The power of women has been completely
broken. At the end of V. v, as the distraught Margaret is led away,
the new King Edward turns his mind to home:

let's away to London
And see our gentle Queen how well she fares:
By this, I hope, she hath a son for me.

(V. v. 86–8)

Lady Gray, now Queen Elizabeth, has no power whatsoever outside the boudoir. Her task is to produce sons for her husband, and the most she can do is to procure preferment at court for members of her own family. The age of warrior maidens and queens has very definitely ended, and it is the Machiavellian Richard who will rise to control all those around him.

The fourth play in the cycle that spans the Wars of the Roses is *Richard III*, one of the most popular of Shakespeare's plays, of which there were no less than six quartos before it was included in the Folio of 1623. Unlike the three parts of *Henry VI*, *Richard III* is structured principally around the figure of the usurping king. It is one of Shakespeare's longest plays and contains a magnificent, meaty part for a male actor, a part originally played by Richard Burbage.

The women in *Richard III* serve as a kind of chorus; there is Queen Margaret, widow of Henry VI and a defeated military opponent, Queen Elizabeth, widow of Edward IV and mother to the children murdered in the Tower by Richard, Lady Anne, the woman who becomes his wife, and the Duchess of York, Richard's own mother. The language of the women takes on an almost ritual quality, particularly apparent in IV. iv, when Margaret, Elizabeth and the Duchess of York list the monstrous deeds of Richard as murderer of their children. When Richard appears they hurl curses at him, but he manages to make them appear almost absurd by his blunt, comic language that is in such stark contrast to theirs, and as soon as the older women have gone, he starts to persuade Elizabeth to grant him her daughter as his second wife. It is hardly surprising that so many critics have traced the figure of Richard back to the Vice of earlier Tudor drama, the character who speaks in the language of the common man and who reminds us continually that the play is merely a game. The women in *Richard III* are the butt of Richard's jokes, they are manipulated and abused by him, rendered powerless and made to appear pathetic and laughable.

If *Richard III* depicts women as marginalised, swept aside by the force of an evil will, the three parts of *Henry VI* offer examples of what women ought not to be, of aberrant feminine behaviour. Disorder and chaos in state affairs are mirrored by disorder in sexual relations. The warrior virgin turns out to be a witch, the wife of an aspiring Duke has ideas above her station and uses witchcraft to achieve her ends, the evil genius of Henry's court is his French queen, the unfaithful Margaret, and the stupidly unaware Edward marries for lust and jeopardises relations with France.

Women in the three parts of *Henry VI* represent disorder, animality, deceit, disloyalty, with the strongest criticism directed against women who fight and women who consort with witches and devils. Given what we know about the great popularity of these plays, it can be deduced that such attitudes must have found considerable public response, no doubt in part due to the way in which they reproduced contemporary issues. The references to disloyal foreign queens, to lands being given as bride-price, to thoughtless marriage, to women at the head of armies and the use of witchcraft for political ends all had their counterparts, real or imaginary, in contemporary public life. And if, as is generally accepted, Elizabeth I was angered by what she saw as a portrayal of herself in the character of Richard II (*c.* 1595) it seems unlikely that topical allusions in the Henry plays would have been any less obvious. There is strong anti-Catholicism in the treatment of Joan la Pucelle, and strong anti-feminism in the treatment of maidens, wives and queens, a tendency that is continued in *Richard III*.

The simplest and crudest picture of the treatment of women in the three parts of *Henry VI* is that women in public life are untrustworthy and should not be given the chance to abuse the power of office. In the disorder of a society at war with itself, women who do not conform to models of proper womanly behaviour are seen as prime sources of increased chaos. This is a classic misogynist position, and certainly found utterance through the pamphleteers of the late sixteenth and early seventeenth centuries. Elizabeth can hardly have been flattered by the portrayal of different aspects of womanhood in these plays, nor by their popularity.

In 1589, writing to Walter Raleigh about *The Faerie Queene*, Spenser says:

In that Faerie Queene I mean Glory in my generall intention,
but in my particular I conceive the most excellent and glorious
person of our soveraine the Queene, and her kingdom in
Faerie Land. . . . For considering she beareth two persons, the
one of a most royal Queene or Empresse, the other of a most
vertuous and beautifull lady, this latter part in some places I
do express in Belphoebe.[6]

He perceives Elizabeth as a split entity; she is sovereign and
she is woman, and these parts form a whole. Whereas kingly
qualities and manliness consistently run together in Shakespeare,
as for a good many other Renaissance writers, the case of a
female ruler was different, for her femininity was often seen as
distinct from her public role, and the two parts could only
uneasily be reconciled.

The harsh economic and political realities of the last three
decades of the sixteenth century effectively ended humanist
social idealism. One such ideal, involving an enlightened
attitude to the education, status and role of women, was dying
long before Elizabeth herself died. The process of glorifying
Elizabeth was linked to a process of denying her femininity,
wherein she was elevated to some kind of higher than earthly
status, transformed into an archetype instead of a woman. Yet
Elizabeth the woman painted her face and wore wigs to the end,
in an effort to be seen to be still a desirable member of her sex
and remind people that she still had 'feminine' qualities.

In his history of sexuality, Michel Foucault has looked at ways
in which sex became invisible and hidden, just as sources of
power and authority also became invisible. He traces this from
the seventeenth century, linking the process to the rise of
rationalism.[7] It would seem, however, that the process was well
under way in England at least in the sixteenth century, and that
the ambiguity surrounding the representations of Elizabeth
testifies to this. Shakespeare's female characters in the three parts
of *Henry VI* typify the changed attitude to women and public
power in an age of diminished ideals.

2
A Range of Voices:
Titus Andronicus and
Love's Labour's Lost

Not all Shakespeare's plays have been as frequently read and performed, nor as greatly admired as others. The list of great tragedies, for example, never includes *Titus Andronicus*, just as the list of favourite comedies never includes *Love's Labour's Lost*. Indeed, both these plays have been the target of considerable critical hostility, and it is worthwhile to consider why this should have been so, particularly when they are so very different in tone and in content, despite the fact that both were probably written within eighteen months to two years of one another. *Titus Andronicus* appeared in print in 1594, but may have been written as early as 1592, while *Love's Labour's Lost* was probably written in 1593–4, though published in 1598, the first of Shakespeare's playtexts to carry his name on its title page.

Dislike of *Titus Andronicus* has been indisputable. Writing in 1780, Ulrich Bräker described it as 'a terrible, appalling, cruel, diabolical play', adding that he could not imagine what class of people 'might look with pleasure at such barbarous games'.[1] This view seems to accord with that of both previous and subsequent generations; the play was long regarded as being in the worst possible taste, with its scenes of horror, such as the rape and mutilation of Lavinia, and serving Tamora her sons, baked in a piecrust at a banquet. This apparent lapse of taste was sometimes explained away by suggestions that *Titus Andronicus* was either not written by Shakespeare at all, or else was a piece of juvenile folly, a play on which he cut his dramatic teeth and which he would no doubt later have preferred to forget. Yet neither of these explanations can be sustained. *Titus Andronicus* is not a play of Shakespeare's extreme youth; it was written after the highly successful three parts of *Henry VI* that had established Shakespeare's reputation, and the play is full of echoes that recur in other plays of his, thereby proving that if he were not the sole author, he certainly had a major hand in it.

The problem is once again one of perspective; later generations have had difficulty in accepting the combination of barbarity and refinement that was part of sixteenth-century life. The distinctions we take for granted in our post-Enlightenment age did not hold true for Renaissance man, who could accept that a mathematician might also be a magician and an astrologer without sullying the good name of science, and who could admire the symmetry and scent of a well-ordered herb garden whilst on his way to watch a public execution.

The public execution provides a useful key for reading the scenes of extreme violence in *Titus Andronicus*. If we take two of the most significant examples of brutal punishment that were administered, in public, in Shakespeare's lifetime, then one of the most striking features of both is their theatricality. The first, in 1579, involved the dismemberment of John Stubbs and his printer who had offended the queen by their pamphlet attacking her proposed marriage with the Duke of Alençon in 1579. There was strong opposition to the sentence – which condemned both men to lose their right hands – since they had articulated feelings shared by a good many people in the country, and those feelings of outrage increased when the two men addressed the crowds from the scaffold. Stubbs is reported to have made a joke, asking the people to pray for him 'now my calamity is at hand', and then after his hand had been cut off, he lifted his hat off his head with his left hand and shouted 'God save the Queen', before dropping to the ground in a faint. The printer was equally brave and equally patriotic, crying 'I have left there a true Englishman's hand!' as he raised his bleeding arm for the people to see.

Two years later, in 1581, at the hanging, drawing and quartering of Edmund Campion, the first Catholic missionary priest to suffer under the harsh law forbidding the dissemination of Catholicism, the crowd were far less sympathetic. Whilst they had stood in disapproving silence as Stubbs's punishment was carried out, they joined in the persecution of Campion with enthusiastic exuberance. It was only the intervention of someone (presumably with royal orders) who insisted that Father Campion be hanged until he was dead that deprived the bloodthirsty anti-Catholic crowd of the full spectacle of the disembowelling of a living body. In later ages, when tastes did not run to such full public spectacles, it is easy to see why a play such as *Titus Andronicus* failed to capture the public imagination.

The fortune of *Love's Labour's Lost* has also not been particularly good, and it has only really come back into favour in the twentieth century. Hazlitt thought it was probably the one play by Shakespeare that he could do without[2] and others have questioned the apparent poverty of plot, the way in which the lovers are more or less interchangeable, the deficiencies and inconsistencies of characterisation and the way in which the play appears to be no more than an extended set of word-games. However, Coleridge (in 1818) was kind to the play, noting that it prefigures many of Shakespeare's later characters with Berowne and Rosaline precursors of Beatrice and Benedick in *Much Ado About Nothing* and Costard of the Tapster in *Measure for Measure*. He also makes an astute comment about the topicality of the play for an Elizabethan audience:

> This sort of story, too, was admirably suited to Shakespeare's times, when the English court was still the foster-mother of the state, and the muses; and when, in consequence, the courtiers and men of rank and fashion, affected a display of wit, point and sententious observation that would be deemed intolerable at present – but which a hundred years of controversy, involving every great political and every dear domestic interest, had trained all but the lowest classes to participate.[3]

Love's Labour's Lost, as has been pointed out, in particular by R. V. David in his prefatory remarks to the Arden edition of the play,[4] has its source in historical fact. There were indeed embassies sent from France to Navarre, and one of these included Marguerite de Valois, the French princess who was also well known as a writer (the first translation of a complete work that Elizabeth I undertook, as a child of eleven, was an English version of Marguerite de Valois's *The Mirror of a Sinful Soul*). Marguerite's brother was the Duc d'Alençon whose attempt to marry Elizabeth so inflamed John Stubbs that he wrote his subversive pamphlet. The real King of Navarre did indeed set up an academy in his court, consisting of learned and serious young men, following a trend favoured among Renaissance courts elsewhere in Europe.

The extent to which Shakespeare modelled his King of Navarre's academy on that of the real King of Navarre is a moot point, and it is not clear how far fact and fiction blend in the play, but what we can assume is that to a greater extent than with many other of his comedies, *Love's Labour's Lost* is a text *à clef*, full of contemporary allusions and possibly even contemporary portraits. The satirical passages would no doubt have delighted an audience familiar with some of the more extreme examples of courtly verse popular among the Euphuists, led by John Lyly. Here, for example, is the extreme case of the ludicrous letter from Don Armado:

> By heaven, that thou art fair, is most infallible; true, that thou art beauteous; truth itself, that thou art lovely. More fairer than fair, beautiful than beauteous, truer than truth itself, have commiseration on thy heroical vassal! The magnanimous and most illustrate king Cophetua set eye upon the pernicious and indubitate beggar Zenelophon, and he it was that might rightly say, *veni, vidi, vici*; which to anatomize in the vulgar (O base and obscure vulgar!) *videlicet*, he came, saw, and overcame: he came, one; saw, two; overcame, three. Who came? the king: why did he come? to see: why did he see? to overcome. To whom came he? to the beggar: what saw he? the beggar: who overcame he? the beggar. (IV. sc. i. 61–75)

And so the letter goes on, prompting the Princess at the end of it to ask 'What plume of feathers is he that indited this letter?'

(IV. i. 95) a deflating comment that carries as much weight in contemporary productions as it surely did when first spoken.

Despite the mixed critical response to both plays, they have attracted the interest of twentieth-century directors, particularly in the 1970s and 1980s. *Love's Labour's Lost* has been performed more frequently than *Titus Andronicus* (though there was a major touring production with Laurence Olivier as Titus and Vivien Leigh as Lavinia in 1955). In 1987 Deborah Warner staged a very successful *Titus Andronicus* at Stratford-upon-Avon, thereby laying to rest the myth that a woman director would be too squeamish to deal with such an explicitly violent play. In 1989 Peter Weiss mounted a production in Rome, using an Italian translation by Agostino Lombardo.

The question of why these two very different plays that were marginal for so long (and still are, to a large extent) should have once again found responsive audiences is an interesting one. One possibility is that since the advent of the horror movie, with its explicit spilling of blood and guts and its depiction of extremes of human behaviour, there is once again a convention into which a play like *Titus Andronicus* can be put. The ages of Illuminism, of Romanticism and of Modernism may have found such writing in bad taste, but in the age of post-Modernism there are fewer illusions about the capacity of human beings for brutality and less surprise at seeing those extremes within the frame of an art-form. Moreover, we need to remember that *Titus Andronicus* was a popular play in its own time and that in some respects it prefigures later plays such as *Othello* (there are strong similarities between Aaron and Iago, and interestingly Aaron is a Moor like Othello), *Macbeth* and *King Lear*. The horror of the murder of Lady Macduff and her children, the blinding of Gloucester, the strangling of the innocent Desdemona are all scenes of great violence, as atrocious as any of those in *Titus Andronicus*. What marks *Titus Andronicus* out as somehow different, as perhaps more extreme, is the same quality that marks some horror movies such as the cult *Nightmare on Elm Street* movies – the fusion of blood-letting, sexual atrocity, revenge and mutilation with grotesque comedy. It is a quality similar to that which prompted W. B. Yeats's remark about the Savage God after seeing Jarry's *Ubu Roi*, another piece many judged to be beyond all the bounds of good taste in theatre. This blend of barbarity and knockabout, almost farcical comedy is reminiscent of medieval drama, of plays such as the Chester Nailers pageant, where the men nailing Christ to the cross swap jokes with one another, or the figure of Herod, a comic monster who arouses gales of laughter until the moment when the slaughter of the Innocents takes place. In act IV of *Titus Andronicus*, for example, Tamora, described by Lavinia just before her rape and mutilation by Tamora's sons as a 'beastly creature, the blot and enemy to our general name' (II. iii. 182–3), has given birth to another child. The child's father, however, is not her husband, the weak Emperor Saturninus, but her lover, Aaron the Moor, and in consequence the baby is black. The Nurse and Aaron discuss the situation – if the Emperor finds out about her adultery, he will have Tamora executed. Aaron asks the nurse how many women saw the child being born, and then the scene suddenly changes in mood and talk turns into savage action:

AARON: But say again, how many saw the child?
NURSE: Cornelia the midwife, and myself,
    And no one else but the delivered empress.
AARON: The empress, the midwife, and yourself:
    Two may keep counsel when the third's away:
    Go to the empress; tell her this I said. [*He kills her*]
    'Wheak, wheak!'
    So cries a pig prepared to the spit.

(IV. ii. 140–7)

A discussion about what to do turns abruptly into a killing, but the murder of the Nurse is accompanied by a joke about stuck pigs squealing, and the horror is thus deconstructed, the brutality turned into black comedy.

Later, in act V, the sense of black comedy becomes even more acute when Titus prepares his revenge and we come to the bloody finale of Shakespeare's bloodiest play. Titus by now has lost everything – his sons have been beheaded, his daughter raped and her hands and tongue cut off, another son has been banished, he has lost his own right hand and the emperor has married Tamora, whose hatred of Titus has precipitated all these catastrophes. In II. i his brother Marcus Andronicus lists the disasters that have befallen him, and is astonished when Titus

laughs. He asks how he can laugh faced with such a list of
torments, and Titus answers:

> Why, I have not another tear to shed:
> Besides, this sorrow is an enemy,
> And would usurp upon my wat'ry eyes,
> And make them blind with tributary tears:
> Then which way shall I find Revenge's cave?
>
> (III. i. 266–70)

In V. ii Tamora and her sons attempt to hound Titus even further,
to drive him beyond the limits of sanity altogether; they go to
visit him in disguise, and Tamora tells him that she is Revenge
in person, accompanied by Rape and Murder,

> sent from th'infernal kingdom
> To ease the gnawing vulture of thy mind.
>
> (V. ii. 31–2)

They mock Titus gleefully, believing him to be completely mad
by now, but Titus is merely biding his time. A feeling of com-
plicity begins to build up between the old man seeking revenge
and the audience who sense that this time Tamora and her sons
have gone too far and are about to get what they deserve.
Tamora believes she is such a good actress she has fooled him
completely, but we can hear from the irony of Titus's speech that
it is he who is actually in control:

> TAMORA: Whate'er I forge to feed his brain-sick humours,
>   Do you uphold and maintain in your speeches
>   For now he firmly takes me for Revenge . . .
>   . . . See, here he comes, and I must ply my theme.
>   [*Enter Titus*]
> TITUS: Long have I been forlorn, and all for thee:
>   Welcome, dread Fury, to my woeful house:
>   Rapine and Murder, you are welcome too.
>   How like the Empress and her sons you are.
>   Well are you fitted, had you but a Moor:
>   Could not all hell afford you such a devil?
>
> (V. ii. 71–3; 80–6)

The moment Tamora leaves, Titus strikes. Chiron and Demetrius her sons are killed by Titus himself, his daughter Lavinia holding a bowl to catch the blood, clutching it between her stumps:

> You know your mother means to feast with me,
> And calls herself Revenge, and thinks me mad.
> Hark, villains, I will grind your bones to dust,
> And with your blood and it I'll make a paste,
> And of the paste a coffin I will rear
> And make two pasties of your shameful heads,
> And bid that strumpet, your unhallowed dam,
> Like to the earth swallow her own increase.
> (V. iii. 84–191)

In the concluding scene of the play, Titus appears at the feast 'like a cook', and explains his choice of costume, in answer to the emperor's query, by saying that he wants to ensure that all goes well with the entertainment. By now the scene is Grand Guignol – the empress eats her own children, Lavinia is killed by her father, who then stabs Tamora. The emperor kills Titus and is then killed in turn by Titus's surviving son, Lucius. The atrocities are completed by the brutal execution of Aaron that is proposed by Lucius.

Later, with Lear's madness, the blinding of Gloucester and Iago's unrepentant end after bringing about the destruction of Othello and Desdemona, Shakespeare was to return to some of the elements already present in *Titus Andronicus*, but with one major difference – an absence of the black comedy. Yet it is the presence of the comic elements that makes *Titus Andronicus* in some respects a very modern play, in the sense that it can be read by contemporary audiences and accepted by them in ways that were not open to earlier audiences.

The genre of the horror movie (and it should be remembered that writers of horror fiction have been consistently in the best-seller lists throughout the 1970s and 1980s) thus provides contemporary audiences with a way of approaching *Titus Andronicus*. Similarly, a change of attitude towards the role of women in society, brought about by the revitalised feminist movements from the 1960s onwards has opened the way for a new reading of *Love's Labour's Lost*, which may partly explain the renewed popularity of the play.

The story of the play is straightforward: a group of young intellectuals led by the King of Navarre decide to live an ascetic life for a three-year period. They plan to study, to live frugally and simply, and to keep to a rule of extreme chastity, not even seeing or speaking to women; or, as Berowne, the least enthusiastic among the men, puts it: 'Not to see ladies, study, fast, not sleep' (I. i. 48). The terms of their agreement are presented in the opening scene of the play and straight away it becomes apparent that they will not be able to keep to the rules, for no sooner have they agreed the terms, than Berowne reminds them that the Princess of France is about to arrive and that the king will have to speak with her. 'Why this was quite forgot', says the king, taken aback by this sudden blow to his carefully constructed plans, to which Berowne retorts: 'So study evermore is overshot' (I. i. 140-1).

The proposed rules of the academy are not very radical; they simply restate the traditional medieval notion of scholarly study and asceticism as an ideal combination, but in this play those rules are presented as absurd and exaggerated, because they are disconnected from the real world. The young men appear as idealistic idiots, who no sooner set up a system that involves commitment to a cause, than circumstances force them to abandon it and break their vows. No sooner have they sworn, than they are foresworn, and are, in their own way, as foolish as the clowns of the play: Don Adriano de Armado, 'a fantastical Spaniard', Holofernes the schoolmaster, Dull the constable, and Costard the clown. The women, in contrast, are sensible and sensitive, as is apparent from their first appearance. They are morally superior and in the exchanges of wit that follow, they also appear as intellectually superior. Finally, in the last scene of the play, they become the controllers, establishing the terms on which the men will be able to win their love.

The four men all fall in love with the women, but as the Princess tells the King in V. ii:

> We have receiv'd your letters full of love;
> Your favours, the ambassadors of love;
> And in our maiden council, rated them

At courtship, pleasant jest, and courtesy,
As bombast and as lining to the time.
                                          (V. ii. 767–73)

The council of women has judged the men's intentions to be
frivolous, and in order for them to be taken seriously, they have
to undergo a test of their constancy. The tone of the play changes
in the final act, as we learn of the death of the princess's father
and the game-playing comes to an end. She tells the king quite
openly that she does not trust his oath, and before she leaves to
begin a twelve-month period of mourning, she tells her beloved
to retire to 'some forlorn and naked hermitage,/Remote from all
the pleasures of the world' for an equal period. Katharine and
Maria impose similar periods of penance on their lovers,
Dumaine and Longaville, while Rosaline orders Berowne to
spend his twelve months in a hospital, visiting the 'speechless
sick'. Berowne comments ironically:

Our wooing doth not end like an old play;
Jack hath not Jill: these ladies' courtesy
Might well have made our sport a comedy.
                                          (V. ii. 865–7)

Muriel Bradbrook has argued that the large number of female
roles in the play suggest that it was written for private
production with a boys' company.[5] Certainly there are an
unusual number of women's parts in this play, and the women
are presented as superior beings. The element of satire, which
has been discussed by a great many critics, is clearly directed at
both individuals and at literary and scholastic trends, and in
contrast to *Titus Andronicus*, this play was presumably written for
a very specific audience, an audience that would have been able
to share the in-jokes and follow Shakespeare's carefully directed
barbed jokes in the direction they were intended to go.
   It is still widely held that the Elizabethan public theatres
attracted two kinds of people: the nobility and members of the
educated classes, and the so-called 'groundlings', who paid a
minimal sum in order to stand in the open yard just below the
stage. This view, which is still regularly repeated in students'
essays, is extremely simplistic and, as Peter Thompson puts it so

succinctly: 'It is quite inconceivable that the great plays of the Elizabethan and Jacobean eras had to reach the discerning audience across an intervening mob of noisy, ignorant yobbos.'[6] He also points out that there is no evidence that it was socially demeaning to stand among the groundlings, nor is there evidence that the groundlings were particularly unruly. Our knowledge of Elizabethan theatre audiences is also very much based on surmise, and the tendency is to read the past through the present, that is, to impose the class consciousness of one age onto another. This kind of facile reading would therefore assume that *Titus Andronicus*, with its camp horrors and its exaggeration would appeal primarily to the groundling, imagined as an Elizabethan variant of the football hooligan. Such an assumption is as wrong as it is absurd.

What we can say with some conviction is that *Love's Labour's Lost* was written for a specific public, while *Titus Andronicus* was written for the wider, general public, but although the specific audience may well have been limited to intellectuals and courtiers, it would be foolish to assume that members of the same group did not also make up a sizeable proportion of the public audiences. Moreover, *Titus Andronicus* has its source in classical literature. Just as *The Comedy of Errors* is based on Plautus, so *Titus Andronicus* is influenced by Seneca and by Ovid. As Kenneth Muir points out, the influence of classical Roman models is consistent with the taste of the age, and he disagrees with Coleridge's disparaging remarks about the play being intended for the vulgar rabble, suggesting that 'Shakespeare was trying by his Senecan horrors to please not the groundlings but what Gabriel Harvey called "the wiser sort".'[7] It is possible to see both *Love's Labour's Lost* and *Titus Andronicus* as plays with intellectual appeal, written by a man with a decent education and an eagerness to experiment with a range of different literary modes and theatrical conventions.

Shakespeare's output is balanced between comedy and tragedy, with plays written for different kinds of actors. But even in two plays as superficially different as *Titus Andronicus* and *Love's Labour's Lost*, there are certain thematic similarities, and those same themes were to return later in other plays.

Both plays are about the disruption of harmonious social order. In *Titus Andronicus* this disruption is very obvious, and the

imagery of mutilation and of metamorphosis that runs throughout the play reinforces the theme. The state of Rome has turned
rotten, the emperor is corrupt, the influence of a foreign power
has warped his judgement. When the last of the killing is completed with the assassination of Saturninus, Marcus Andronicus
makes an appeal to the citizens for a new order of things:

> You sad fac'd men, people and sons of Rome,
> By uproars sever'd, as a flight of fowl
> Scatter'd by winds and high tempestuous gusts,
> O let me teach you how to knit again
> This scattered corn into one mutual sheaf,
> These broken limbs again into one body;
> Lest Rome herself be bane unto herself,
> And she whom mighty kingdoms curtsy to,
> Like a forlorn and desperate castaway,
> Do shameful execution on herself.
>
> (V. iii. 67–76)

Corruption in the state, a society in the process of poisoning
itself is a theme that recurs in a great many of Shakespeare's
plays. Sometimes, as in *Titus Andronicus*, that corruption destroys
innocent individuals caught up in its coils, whilst in *King Lear* or
in *Measure for Measure*, for example, we see how the social order
collapses when authority figures are weak, misguided or foolish.

Love's Labour's Lost offers a comic parallel, as the King of
Navarre tries to enforce a vow of chastity that he is incapable of
keeping. In the first scene of the play where Berowne reluctantly
agrees to keep to the rules of the academy there is a reference to
the tearing out of tongues, an image that becomes brutal reality
in *Titus Andronicus*:

BEROWNE [*Reads*]: 'Item: that no woman shall come within a
    mile of my court' – Hath this been proclaimed?
LONGAVILLE: Four days ago.
BEROWNE: Let's see the penalty – 'on pain of losing her
    tongue'. Who devised this penalty?
LONGAVILLE: Marry, that did I.
BEROWNE: Sweet lord, and why?

LONGAVILLE: To fright them hence with that dread penalty.
BEROWNE: A dangerous law against gentility!
'Item: if any man be seen to talk with a woman within the
term of three years, he shall endure such public shame as
the rest of the court can possibly devise.' –
This article, my liege, yourself must break;

(I. i. 119–32)

Berowne reminds the king of the imminent visit of the French
princess and so the attempt to impose a rigorous rule of chastity
is immediately doomed. That such a law is anti-nature is
emphasised by the songs that conclude the play, compiled, as
Armado explains, by two learned men in praise of the owl and
the cuckoo. The songs also remind us of the harsher realities
behind idealised visions of Arcadia, for the cuckoo 'mocks
married men' in spring, while in winter even a fair maiden's
nose 'looks red and raw'. The King of Navarre and his companions are guilty of having been out of touch with the real
world and with the regenerating forces of nature and of love,
forces to which the women in the play are clearly much more
closely attached.

Love's Labour's Lost is a play in which language predominates.
It is made up of a series of games, all of which involve different
registers, from the absurd pedantry of the schoolmaster to the
linguistic excesses of Don Armado and the pseudo-Petrarchan
language of the courtiers. Berowne, who is a master of stylistic
devices, even tries to fool Rosaline with an apparently new-
found down-to-earth style, but she swiftly puts him down in the
following exchange:

BEROWNE: Taffeta phrases, silken terms precise,
    Three-pil'd hyperboles, spruce affection . . .
    I do foreswear them . . .
    Henceforth my wooing mind shall be express'd
    In russet yeas and honest kersey noes:
    And to begin: Wench – so God help me, law! –
    My love to thee is sound, sans crack or flaw.
ROSALINE: Sans 'sans', I pray you.

(V. ii. 406–7; 410; 412–16)

In *Titus Andronicus* the games are deadly; Lavinia is raped and mutilated, the perpetrators of the outrage meet grotesquely horrible deaths. The laughter that accompanies some of these excesses is not light-hearted; it is diabolical laughter, and its function is similar to that of Brecht's *Verfremdungseffekt* – it both distances the audience from the emotionality of what is going on immediately in front of their eyes and at the same time it underlines the horror of it all. Titus in his cook's uniform is not a figure of fun; he is a ghastly personification of Revenge, and the fact that his disguise may be comical only reinforces that image.

Both *Titus Andronicus* and *Love's Labour's Lost* are plays that deal with potential social disintegration, but from totally different perspectives. In the one case, that disintegration takes place and the play ends with an order for Tamara's body to be thrown to wild beasts and birds of prey. There is no concluding vision of harmony, only the hope that with a new ruler and a new generation of Romans, personified in young Lucius, Titus's grandson, the atrocious past can be overcome. In the case of *Love's Labour's Lost* there is no comic resolution either; instead, there is a promise of future happiness if the lovers can remain constant for the time prescribed. Jack does not have Jill and the play concludes with the lovers about to part for some considerable time.

Although these two plays are by no means the earliest examples of Shakespeare's work as a writer of comedy and tragedy, they nevertheless show some of the ways in which he was trying out forms and experimenting with different genres. They provide a useful touchstone for approaching the plays of the remaining years of Elizabeth's reign, for each in its own way is an exaggeration. *Love's Labour's Lost* is palpably a play for an élite audience, a satirical in-joke, something perhaps not unlike a university review of today. *Titus Andronicus* has great tragic potential but goes too far into conventional grotesque. Both plays are somehow slightly off-balance, the pace of action in each of them moves the plot along at the expense of such characterisation, and indeed in both these plays character is secondary to the narrative line. But *Titus Andronicus* is a great deal more than a third-rate entertainment for a bloodthirsty mob, and *Love's Labour's Lost* is more than just an in-joke. Both plays show a playwright in the process of finding more of his several voices. Shakespeare had already written the three parts of *Henry VI* and *Richard III* by the time he wrote *Titus Andronicus,* and had also tried his hand at comedy with *The Comedy of Errors, The Taming of the Shrew* and *Two Gentlemen of Verona.* Moreover, between 1592 and 1594 he wrote his two narrative poems, *Venus and Adonis* and *The Rape of Lucrece.* All this activity testifies to a desire to try out new forms, to play with the play itself, and both *Titus Andronicus* and *Love's Labour's Lost* deserve less hostile responses than they have so often been accorded by both critics and directors until recent times.

3
The Prison and the World: *Richard III*

Shakespeare's history plays consist of two tetralogies: the first comprises the three parts of *Henry VI*, with *Richard III* continuing the story up to the Battle of Bosworth in 1485, when Richard was defeated by Richmond, who then became Henry VII, the first Tudor king and grandfather of Elizabeth. The second tetralogy returns to an earlier historical period, from 1398 to 1420, and consists of the two parts of *Henry IV* and *Henry V*, preceded by *Richard II*, the play that recounts the coming to power of Henry IV when, as Henry Bolingbroke, Duke of Hereford, he is instrumental in the deposition of Richard. Although not written in chronological sequence, these eight plays do cover a continuous period of turbulent English history, tracing the rise and fall of successive rulers through the period of the Hundred Years War and the War of the Roses.

One interesting development with these eight plays in recent years has been the number of chronological stagings, with the plays presented as a sequence, beginning with *Richard II* and running through to *Richard III*. This means that the plays are perceived as component parts in an epic cycle, and the fact that they are often staged chronologically changes the way in which they are interpreted. This sense of an epic sequence also means that the ninth history play, *King John*, written after *Richard II* (1585) and before the two parts of *Henry IV* (1597–8), has been somewhat marginalised, an interesting shift in perceptions, since the play enjoyed considerable success in the nineteenth century.

The tendency to see the tetralogies as two clear units, virtually as two halves of a whole cycle means that contemporary audiences tend to read the plays as dramatisations of historical facts. There must be many members of the public worldwide who learned all they know about the Wars of the Roses or the French wars from Shakespeare's treatment of Holinshead's material. But for Elizabethan audiences, the history plays, including *King John*, brought topical issues onto the stage. The plays were carefully structured to focus on some particular aspect of the central theme of them all: a debate on the nature of kingship, what it means to be a good king, and what the relationship should be between ruler and the state. Elizabethan audiences would have had some knowledge of the historical background, enough probably to enable them to make connections between past and present. Today, in contrast, our central concern is for the characters, for Richard II in his downfall, for Richard III in his megalomania, for devious King John and the opportunistic Bastard, for young Prince Hal who learns how to rule and becomes the hero of Agincourt.

The history plays enjoyed various degrees of success, but *Richard II* was so popular that it was printed three times in two years. The play was also seen as particularly controversial, and Queen Elizabeth is said to have protested that she was well aware that she was supposed to be represented in the figure of the deposed king. Throughout her lifetime the deposition scene was censored and omitted from all published versions. In 1601, on the eve of the abortive rising led by the Earl of Essex, his friends paid the Lord Chamberlain's men to stage the play, an action viewed as particularly provocative. The content of the play was political dynamite at such a time, and the implications of Richard's words cannot have been lost on the contemporary audience when he calls for a mirror, after Bolingbroke has taken the crown from him, and reflects upon the illusory nature of power:

> Was this the face
> That every day under his household roof
> Did keep ten thousand men? Was this the face

That like the sun did make beholders wink?
Was this the face which faced so many follies,
That was at last outfaced by Bolingbroke?
A brittle glory shineth in this face.
As brittle as the glory is the face,
[*Smashes the glass*]
For there it is, cracked in a hundred shivers.

(IV. i. 282–90)

Like *Richard III*, the play recounts how a throne was lost and won, but in contrast to that earlier success, in *Richard II*, Shakespeare focuses on the complexities of determining what may constitute good or bad kingship. Richard III is a monster, a Machiavellian who schemes and muders to obtain the crown and then rules as a tyrant. It is with a sense of relief that the audience welcomes his overthrow, for despite the comic features that serve to redeem him slightly, he becomes progressively more bloody as his reign continues. He is overthrown by the future Henry VII, as Shakespeare followed convention by proclaiming the Tudors as saviours of the realm.

Richard II offers a portrait of a king who rules unwisely, rather than cruelly, and who is transformed into a figure of great tragic stature when the moment of his enforced abdication arrives. The inconsistencies of Richard's character serve to heighten the debate on the nature and right of kingship which lies at the heart of the play. Richard's principle crime is that of being too easily influenced, of failing to assert authority independently. The dying Gaunt accuses him:

And thou, too careless patient as thou art,
Commit'st thy anointed body to the cure
Of those physicians that first wounded thee.
A thousand flatterers sit within thy crown
Whose compass is no bigger than thy head,
And yet encaged in so small a verge
The waste is no whit lesser than thy land.

(II. i. 97–103)

Gaunt believes that Richard has allowed himself to be governed by others, by men such as Bushy and Bagot, described by

Bolingbroke as 'the caterpillars of the commonwealth', and when he captures and executes them, Bolingbroke accuses both men of having misled the king, and of having exercised such influence over him that they caused a breach between Richard and his queen, an implicit suggestion of Richard's possible homosexuality that is not developed elsewhere, but which may be linked to the explicit homosexuality of Marlowe's rival play, *Edward II*.[1]

The image of waste, of a garden run to seed and infested by caterpillars runs throughout *Richard II*, and in a scene that stands out as a set piece, the sorrowing queen overhears two gardeners talking about their work and about the state of the kingdom. Bushy and Green are now described as 'weeds', sheltered by Richard's broad spreading leaves, who 'seemed in eating him to hold him up'. The gardeners, representative of the common man, compare the task of maintaining a garden prudently, taking care to weed and prune when appropriate, to the task of governing a kingdom. Richard is termed 'the wasteful king', and the men regret that 'he had not so trimmed and dressed his land/As we do this garden' (III. iv. 57–8)

The gardening scene serves several purposes. It represents visually the recurrent imagery of good husbandry, and it also shows the extent to which Bolingbroke's cause has won the sympathy of the common man. The case against Richard is far from being clear-cut, and although we hear a great deal about his inadequacies as a ruler, he is by no means a bloodthirsty tyrant. The grieving queen who overhears the men talking introduces yet another dimension; she is an emblematic figure of mourning, reminiscent of Mary at the foot of the cross, and in this respect her presence ties in with another pattern of imagery that begins to develop as Richard comes under pressure to abdicate, the image of the king as the suffering Christ.

The Richard that appears in the opening scene of the play is a rather petty figure. He is to preside over the quarrel between Bolingbroke and Mowbray and make a judgement in one man's favour, but although he listens to the empassioned speeches of both, he says very little and what he does say is inadequate, both stylistically and in terms of content. He refuses to allow the men to fight to prove their honour in combat, and his speech, in rhymed couplets, is one of the feeblest of the play:

Wrath-kindled gentlemen, be ruled by me.
Let's purge this choler without letting blood.
This we prescribe though no physician,
Deep malice makes too deep incision.
Forget, forgive, conclude and be agreed.
Our doctors say this is no month to bleed.

(I. i. 152–7)

The imagery of husbandry ties in with the imagery of surgery in this play. A good gardener needs to cut back unwanted growth; a good physician must cut away gangrenous flesh, and without such radical treatment neither the plants nor the patient can be saved. The ability to cut back radically is something that Richard does not possess; he shrinks from surgery as he shrinks from the sight of blood being spilled. When Bolingbroke and Mowbray meet for the second time, Richard allows the combatants to put on their armour and step forward to fight, then at the very last minute he stops everything:

For that our kingdom's earth should not be soiled
With that dear blood which it hath fostered,
And for our eyes do hate the dire aspect
Of civil wounds ploughed up with neighbours' sword.

(I. iii. 125–8)

Richard's behaviour towards Bolingbroke and Mowbray is erratic and inappropriate for a king who is also supposed to act as arbiter, but it does not establish grounds for deposition. It is not until the second act that the extent of his unfitness for government begins to be made explicit. He seizes the property of the banished Bolingbroke, and seems unable to understand the arguments of his uncle, the Duke of York, who warns him that by such an action he will lose 'a thousand well-disposed hearts'. Once he has left for Ireland, Ross, Northumberland and Willoughby acting as a chorus, present a litany of Richard's abuses – he is 'basely led by flatterers', he has imposed heavy taxes on the commons 'and quite lost their hearts', alienated the nobility, spent more in peacetime than his ancestors spent on wars, and because of his wastefulness the only way he can finance his war in Ireland is by 'the robbing of the banished duke'.

Critics have frequently pointed to the apparent discrepancy in characterisation between Richard as he appears in the first two acts of the play and his appearances from the third act onwards. The long, lyrical soliloquies that are given to Richard as the process of abdication is set in motion come unexpectedly after the second-rate language he uses earlier. However, to Elizabethan audiences such apparent inconsistency would not have seemed unusual, for it is only in the twentieth century, conditioned as we have been by the impact of naturalist characterisation, that consistency of character has become important. Whatever the Renaissance concept of characterisation may have been, it was not based on pyschological realism as we understand that term today.[2]

In *Richard II*, as in many of Shakespeare's plays, characterisation takes place primarily through language. The play is constructed around a series of almost pageant-like scenes – the challenge, the deathbed, the combat, Richard's return to England, Richard at Flint Castle, the garden, the court, the prison and so forth. There is very little action and until Richard's murder, very little happens on-stage. Almost all the action is reported, and since most of the case against Richard is presented to the audience through the opinions of various characters, language acquires particular importance. Bolingbroke's language is blunt and more homely than Richard's, but although this makes him appear more sympathetic on his first appearance, once Richard's language changes and he embarks on his soliloquies, Bolingbroke seems to lose much of his authority. By the end of the play he is speaking in basic rhyming couplets that recall Richard's own feeble language when he intervened to prevent the combat in act I. Bolingbroke has become king, but like his predecessor he is not certain how to rule, and his language reflects that uncertainty, 'They love not poison that do poison need', says Bolingbroke when faced with the dead body of the murdered Richard. Like Richard, who was unwilling to take a stand and prune the garden of his kingdom, Bolingbroke is unwilling to accept responsibility for killing Richard:

> Though I did wish him dead
> I hate the murderer, love him murdered.
>   (V. vi. 39–40)

The play ends with the new king mourning the old and vowing
to go on a pilgrimage to the Holy Land to atone for the crime
that has been committed.

Act II ends with a short scene between the Earl of Salisbury
and a Welsh captain, exchanging news about the reported death
of the king. When Richard next appears, before Berkeley Castle,
he is transformed; it is as though he has undergone a symbolic
death and been reborn as something other. The Richard who
appears now is in full control of language, and asserts his own
position as ruler with absolute conviction:

> I had forgot myself. Am I not king?
> Awake, thou sluggard majesty! thou sleepest.
> Is not the king's name twenty thousand names?
> Arm, arm my name! A puny subject strikes
> At thy great glory. Look not to the ground.
> Ye favourites of a king, are we not high?
> High be our thoughts.
>   (III. i. 83–9)

In his rebirth or awakening process, Richard is now aware of
the pattern of the world around him. It has often been pointed
out that the play is full of symbolic images of rising and falling,
and the pageant quality of much of the action is reflected in the
rituals of bowing, kneeling, ascending and descending thrones
that run throughout the play. Along with standard Renaissance
images of the sun that is eclipsed, the wheel of fortune and the
scales, are other more familiar metaphors. Bolingbroke ascends
the ladder of ambition to the throne, plants in the garden droop
and leaves fall, and in the very moment when Richard should
hand the crown to Bolingbroke, he clings on to it and compares
himself and the future king to buckets in a well:

> Give me the crown. Here, cousin, seize the crown,
> On this side my hand and on that side thine.
> Now is this golden crown like a deep well

That owes two buckets, filling one another,
The emptier ever dancing in the air,
The other down, unseen and full of water.
That bucket, down and full of tears, am I,
Drinking my griefs whilst you mount up on high.

                                        (IV. i. 181–7)

Stagings of the play cannot avoid the numerous references to ascending and descending that recur consistently, and it is likely that these symbolic images were accentuated in early productions by the use of different levels in the theatre. Shakespeare wrote *Richard II* when the company was still performing at the Theatre in Shoreditch, but after 1596 the company played at the Swan, built in the previous year. Johannes de Witt's famous drawings of the Swan, reproduced by generations of schoolchildren studying the Elizabethan theatre, depicts a multi-level stage, one where the use of split-level scenes (for example Richard on the walls of Flint Castle in act III) would have been particularly effective. Andrew Gurr points out that the only major piece of property required to stage the play was a throne, which would have been set up on a platform, with steps leading to it and covered by a canopy.[3]

The stage representation of kingly power, focused on the throne, reflects the trappings of public power that would have been familiar to the Elizabethan world. *Richard II*, more than any other of Shakespeare's history plays, depicts the physicality of power, and as Richard descends from the battlements, from the throne and ultimately from the public eye, he moves increasingly into a world of confinement:

          I have been studying how I may compare
          This prison where I live unto the word . . .

                                        (V. v. 1–2)

But Richard's descent is paradoxically a spiritual ascent. Like Gloucester, who can say after his blinding 'I stumbled when I saw', so Richard comes to greater self-knowledge and to awareness of his relations to the rest of humanity as he loses his throne. York, describing Richard's humiliation and the triumph of

Bolingbroke, uses the metaphor of the theatre to explain his plight:

> As in a theatre the eyes of men
> After a well-graced actor leaves the stage
> Are idly bent on him that enters next,
> Thinking his prattle to be tedious,
> Even so or with much more contempt men's eyes
> Did scowl on Richard.
>
> (V. ii. 23–8)

Richard's tragedy is personal; in the eyes of the world, the man who is seen to be the most effective ruler holds the stage. When he sat on the throne and gave commands, Richard was visible to all and yet paradoxically also anonymous; being king, he represented kingliness and so was a living icon of himself. Once he is deposed that situation changes, and he begins his journey towards enlightenment.

Once Richard's power is challenged and he regains control over language, he is increasingly compared to Christ on his journey to Calvary. As he is forced to hand over the crown to Bolingbroke, he makes an explicit reference to Christ's betrayal:

> Did they not sometimes cry 'All hail' to me?
> So Judas did to Christ, but he in twelve
> Found truth in all but one, I in twelve thousand none.
>
> (IV. i. 169–71)

while the scene where he is met by the grieving queen as he is being led to prison recalls the meeting between Christ and Veronica. York's account of the contrast between Bolingbroke's triumphal procession into London and Richard's wretched treatment by the mob again recalls the tormenting of Christ by the people who had once cheered him:

> But dust was thrown upon his sacred head,
> Which with such gentle sorrow he shook off,
> His face still combating with tears and smiles,
> The badges of his grief and patience,
> That had not God for some strong purpose steeled

> The hearts of men they must perforce have melted
> And barbarism itself have pitied him
>
> (V. ii. 30–6)

As the Christ parallels increase and Richard becomes a tragic hero, rising like a phoenix from the ashes of the weak, vacillating ruler of the first two acts, so the imagery and structure of the play becomes increasingly concerned with dichotomies. There are two kings, and as the one falls from public grace, so he rises in moral and spiritual stature, while the strong young hero who challenged his cousin's right to rule ascends to the throne, and finds himself dealing with absurd situations such as the dispute between York and his Duchess and forced to become an accessory to murder. Images of light and darkness, of wealth and poverty, of greatness and smallness continue the fundamental theme of contrast, and in his prison speech in act V Richard seeks to 'compare this prison where I live unto the World'. His dying words, as Exton stabs him, take up the contrast between earthly greatness and heavenly greatness, between temporary and eternal life:

> Mount, mount my soul. Thy seat is up on high
> Whilst my gross flesh sinks downward, here to die.
>
> (V. v. 111–12)

The transformation of Richard into a man who is made spiritually noble through suffering demonstrates Shakespeare's skill in manipulating audience sympathy. Bolingbroke, the plain speaker, the blunt man who takes up the sword against the king out of a sense of genuine grievance, is diminished in stature by contrast. We may share Bolingbroke's sense of outrage at Richard's behaviour when he intervenes to forbid the tournament, but by the time Richard appears in prison, a doomed man struggling to understand what life is all about, he has become a man of almost superhuman stature, a figure who has been tragically divorced from his own kingdom ('doubly divorced' is the phrase he uses when separated from his wife, the first divorce being his separation from his crown).

One effect of staging the history plays in a continuous cycle is to change the terms of the debate about kingship and good government that lie at the core of all of them and to make the plays appear closer to Greek tragedy. The death of Richard II becomes a crime that Bolingbroke, now Henry IV, has on his conscience, which then lies like a curse through the two parts of *Henry IV.* The triumph of Henry V, the man who appears to be the saviour of the realm, is followed by the disastrous reign of his son, Henry VI, whose weakness makes possible the accession of a bloodthirsty tyrant, Richard III. This reading suggests that like the House of Atreus, there is a curse on the royal house of England, which is only lifted by the healing hands of the founder of the Tudor dynasty. Richard II is interpreted as a truly tragic hero, a victim whose sufferings cause grief for generations to come.

But this is a twentieth-century reading of the play, and it is a reading that happens when we deliberately change Shakespeare's sequence of writing and presenting the plays, and turn it into a chronological one. Richard does suffer manifestly, and he is compared to Christ, but he is also the proud, intolerant, abusive ruler who drove his subjects, both noble and commoner, into the service of another man. Bolingbroke's fittedness for the throne is not questioned; the play very deliberately does not challenge the rightness of Bolingbroke's cause. Richard III, for example, is a scheming tyrant from the outset, while Macbeth becomes successively more savage, but Bolingbroke appears throughout as a modest man, respected by everyone and loved by the people.

The ambiguity in *Richard II* about the qualities necessary to govern and about the role of the will of the people in challenging an anointed ruler's absolute right must have attributed to the great popularity of the play in the 1590s and to its reputation as a subversive text. Andrew Gurr points out that the position of Richard 'surrounded by bad counsellors and lacking a direct heir', could be related to Elizabeth's own position,[4] while Stephen Greenblatt discusses the Queen's concern that the play was reportedly performed forty times in open streets and houses, arguing that by such public performances the 'conventional containment' of the playhouses ceased to exist and the performance could easily be seen as open provocation.[5] The choice of *Richard II* by the Earl of Essex's supporters is further evidence of the way in which the play was perceived by contemporary audiences, more as a parable than as a tragedy.

Twentieth-century audiences are able to see the fall of Richard within the wider context of Shakespeare's work, and in consequence the play can be linked to the later tragedies in terms of its content and to other more lyrical plays such as *Romeo and Juliet* in terms of language. But an Elizabethan audience, no matter how moved they may have been by Richard's plight, will have felt the strength of Gaunt's words as he accuses Richard of betraying the state and the people:

> Landlord of England art thou now, not king,
> Thy state of law is bondslave to the law.
> (II. i. 113–14)

The now famous notion of Shakespeare as our contemporary is thus seen to be both true and false simultaneously.[6] In so far as he deals with human suffering, Shakespeare is universal; Ulrich Bräker compares Richard's plight to that of the common man in his habitual plain terms:

> Of course the fall is great from a throne into the mire – an insigificant citizen of the world can't fall so far – and the farther you fall, the more it hurts. But there's many a man only fallen from one mire into another and has still howled pitifully enough.[7]

But in so far as he dealt with key political issues of the day through the medium of the drama in its Renaissance context, Shakespeare belonged to the Elizabethan age, and in terms of content, structure and presentation, his work typifies an age that we can only reconstruct through fantasies.

4
Wayward Sons and Daughters: *Romeo and Juliet*, *A Midsummer Night's Dream* and *Henry IV, Part 1*

In his contribution to a collection of new psychoanalytic essays on Shakespeare, C. L. Barber argues that 'Shakespeare's art is distinguished by the intensity of its investment in the human family, and especially in the continuity of the family across generations.'[1] He traces a difference in focus through Shakespeare's opus, suggesting that the earlier plays are characterised by 'a very strong identification of the cherishing role of the parents in early infancy'.[2] Certainly the role of the family and in particular the question of the relationship between children and parents in adolescence is strikingly present in a large number of Shakespeare's plays, particularly those that date from the mid-1590s. This interest cuts across other categories, and in this chapter we shall be looking at a tragedy (*Romeo and Juliet*), a comedy (*A Midsummer Night's Dream*) and a history (*Henry IV, Part 1*) all of which share certain common thematic lines relating to parents and children.

For a long time *Romeo and Juliet* was regarded abroad as one of Shakespeare's best plays. Chateaubriand lists it along with *Macbeth*, *Richard III*, *Othello*, *Julius Caesar* and *Hamlet*. Goethe translated it into German, Ulrich Bräker's naïve verdict lists

Romeo and Juliet, *Hamlet* and *Othello* as Shakespeare's best creations. In England, however, its fortunes were more variable and the play was described by Samuel Pepys as 'the worst that ever I heard in my life'.[3] It seems to be a play that on the one hand has been a great commercial success, since the roles of the young lovers offered an ideal vehicle to star actors from the eighteenth century onwards, but on the other hand has presented critics with the problem of whether it can be considered to be a true tragedy. Certainly, in the Aristotelian sense, *Romeo and Juliet* is not a study of a fall from greatness, and there are strong comic elements present in the play that have often caused problems for directors, some of whom have preferred to omit the clowns and tone down the Nurse's dirty jokes. In fact, the play does not really take on tragic overtones until the start of act III, when Tybalt and Mercutio fight and Mercutio is fatally wounded. The conflict between the Montagus and the Capulets appears more ridiculous than deadly at first, with the ludicrous brawl in the streets of Verona that opens the play and then with the headlong passion of Romeo for Juliet that is presented as decidedly comic. When Friar Lawrence hears of Romeo's sudden love for Juliet, he is astonished:

> Holy Saint Francis, what a change is here!
> Is Rosaline, that thou didst love so dear,
> So soon forsaken? Young men's love then lies
> Not truly in their hearts but in their eyes.
>
> (II. iii. 65–8)

Mercutio puts it just as succinctly, though rather more crudely:

> Oh flesh, flesh, how art thou fishified! Now is he for the numbers that Petrarch flowed in. Laura to his lady was a kitchen wench (marry, she had a better love to berhyme her), Dido a dowdy, Cleopatra a gypsy, Helen and Hero hildings and harlots, Thisbe a grey eye or so, but not to the purpose.
>
> (II. iv. 38–43)

The opposite is the case with *A Midsummer Night's Dream*, which opens on a serious note and then shifts into comedy. Egeus, a righteous Athenian parent, has brought his daughter

Hermia before Duke Theseus to demand that his right as father
to chose a husband for his child be honoured. His complaint
might just as well have been spoken by Juliet's father, had he
known what was going on, for the terms on which Lysander has
won Hermia's love bear a remarkable resemblance to the way in
which Romeo has wooed Juliet:

> Full of vexation come I, with complaint
> Against my child, my daughter Hermia.
> Stand forth Demetrius. My noble lord,
> This man hath my consent to marry her.
> Stand forth Lysander. And, my gracious duke,
> This man hath bewitched the bosom of my child.
> Thou, thou, Lysander, thou hast given her rhymes,
> And interchanged love-tokens with my child:
> Thou hast by moonlight at her window sung,
> With feigning voice, verses of feigning love:
> And stol'n the impression of her fantasy
> With bracelets of thy hair, rings, gauds, conceits,
> Knacks, trifles, nosegays, sweetmeats – messengers
> Of strong prevailment in unhardened youth.
>
> (I. i. 22–35)

Egeus demands the full penalty of the law for Hermia's
disobedience: if she will not marry Demetrius by the allotted
time given her to make up her mind, then she must either die or
be consigned to a closed convent. Theseus warns Hermia that
her father should be obeyed and so the action of the play begins,
based on a potentially deadly situation.

The great Norwegian writer and director Bjørnstjerne Bjørnson said that of all his readings of Shakespeare, *A Midsummer
Night's Dream* made the most powerful impression on him,
because 'it is the richest in fantasy and most innocent work
written by Shakespeare'.[4] This idea of innocence is still very
strong, fuelled by the nineteenth-century taste for whimsical
fairies, and it is significant that this is one of the most frequently
performed plays in schools, on account of its large cast that
enables even the smallest first formers to play Cobweb and
Mustardseed and on account of its seeming harmlessness.

Jan Kott, in contrast, illuminates the darker side of the play.

He points to the devilish origins of the figure of Puck, notes the promiscuity of the fairy king and queen and of both Theseus and his bride Hippolyta, discusses the bestiality of Titania's passion for Bottom and suggests that the play is full of erotic imagery and of unpleasant creatures such as snakes, bats and spiders. His description of fairyland is as remote from Bjørnson's innocent ideal as it is possible to be:

> I imagine Titania's court as consisting of old men and women, toothless and shaking, their mouths wet with saliva, who sniggeringly procure a monster for their mistress . . . in this nightmarish summer night, the ass does not symbolize stupidity. Since antiquity and up to the Renaissance the ass was credited with the strongest sexual potency and among all the quadrupeds is supposed to have the longest and hardest phallus.[5]

In *Henry IV, Part 1*, Prince Henry and Falstaff stage an imaginary discussion between the Prince and his father. Falstaff plays the king at first, praising his 'son's' companion as 'a good portly man . . . of a cheerful look, a pleasing eye and a most noble carriage' (II. iv. 412–13). Then they reverse the roles, with Hal playing his own father, the king, and Falstaff playing Hal. Once he assumes the role of king, Henry is able to attack Falstaff in very strong terms that recall Kott's vision of the decadent fairy court:

> There is a devil haunts thee in the likeness of an old fat man, a tun of man in thy companion. Why dost thou converse with that trunk of humours, that bolting-hutch of beastliness, that swollen parcel of dropsies, that huge bombard of sack, that stuffed cloak-bag of guts, that roasted Manningtree ox with the pudding in his belly, that reverend Vice, that grey Iniquity, that Father Ruffian, that Vanity in years. (II. iv. 435–42)

> . . . That villainous abominable misleader of youth, Falstaff, that old white-bearded Satan. (II. iv. 449–50)

All three plays rest on a balance between comic and tragic elements. *Romeo and Juliet* opens with a pair of fighting clowns

(after the brief Prologue that sets out the plot) and ends with
bereaved parents standing helplessly over their children's
bodies. *A Midsummer Night's Dream* opens with the threat of
death and with a bleak picture of a world thrown into chaos:

> The spring, the summer,
> The childing autumn, angry winter, change
> Their wonted liveries; and the mazed world,
> By their increase, now knows not which is which.
> And this same progeny of evils comes
> From our debate, from our dissension:
> We are their parents and original.
>
> (II. i. 111–17)

Thanks to the intervention of Oberon and Puck with their
magic filtre, order is restored by the end of the play, and the final
act turns tragedy into farce, as the mechanicals stage their
version of the doomed love of Pyramus and Thisbe, a narrative
that bears close resemblance to the tragic errors in the lives of
Romeo and Juliet.

Henry IV, Part 1 gives us the figure of Falstaff, the huge debauched cheerful character that Tolstoy felt was the only natural
and typical character ever created by Shakespeare. David Wiles
believes that the role of Falstaff was created by the great clown
Will Kemp, and suggests that Falstaff should be seen as an
emblem of Carnival, a figure whose power must come to an end
with the advent of Lent that takes us towards the most important
Church festival of the calendar.[6] Falstaff is exposed in two
sequences as a coward and a liar – first in the robbery and then,
more seriously, in the concluding scene of the play when he
attempts to claim that he is responsible for killing Hotspur.
Significantly, although Prince Henry appears to enjoy the first
exposing of Falstaff, he does nothing the second time and Falstaff
appears to have the upper hand. Henry's last words to Falstaff,
spoken in an aside, are ambiguous:

> For my part, if a lie may do thee grace,
> I'll gild it with the happiest terms I have.
>
> (V. v. 156–7)

It is not until the second part of *Henry IV* that Falstaff is finally punished when Prince Henry, now King Henry V, rejects him and abjures his own debauched past life.

There has been a great deal of critical debate about the rejection of Falstaff. Henry is often perceived as cold, as an untrue friend who sets duty before feeling. But this reading fails to take into account the function of Falstaff as a mock father-figure to the Prince. Hal is learning to be a king, and his own father, wracked with guilt at the way in which he acquired the throne in the first place, is an inadequate model for a son to follow. Falstaff takes on that paternal role, but as is very clear in *Henry IV, Part 1*, he is an anti-hero and certainly not a model for any future king. He is the Lord of Misrule, and only by rejecting him can Henry assume full power over and responsibility for his subjects. The scene where Henry and Falstaff play the roles of father and son, face to face is therefore fundamental, because in the two versions of the dialogue we have the two alternatives open to Henry. When Falstaff plays the king, Henry is powerless, for he cannot go against his father and his monarch. But when Henry plays the king, and Falstaff plays Henry, the power invested in the king demands the rejection of misrule, and the errant son can prove himself true at last. Falstaff's banishment is prefigured in his own words, when in the role of Henry, he says 'Banish plump Jack, and banish all the world' and Henry, no longer playing a part, replies: 'I do, I will' (II. iv. 464–6).

The balance between tragic and comic elements in the three plays is not the only similarity. Present in all three is the clash between generations, with parents angry at their children's disobedience and children resentful of their parents' power. Hermia and Egeus are openly at odds with each other, as are Prince Henry and King Henry. In the opening scene of *Henry IV, Part 1*, King Henry compares his son to Northumberland's son, Harry Hotspur, and expresses his wish that a Puck or an Oberon might come forward and say that the two sons had really been exchanged at birth:

> Oh that it could be proved
> That some night-tripping fairy had exchanged
> In cradle-clothes our children where they lay,
> And called mine Percy, his Plantagenet!

Then would I have his Harry, and he mine.
(I. i. 85–9)

Henry's progress from profligacy to kingliness takes effort
and pain. There is no easy solution, no fairy intervention to put
things right overnight. Nor do the fairies intervene in the tragic
downfall of Romeo and Juliet. Mercutio, in his Queen Mab
soliloquy in act I, describes the night-time cunning of a demonic
fairy who brings chaos in human order and nightmares into
human minds. Romeo interrupts his friend with the terse comment 'Thou talk'st of nothing!', for the world of faery has no
place in what Romeo sees as reality. In Romeo's world, fantasy
is subordinate to action: he no sooner sees Juliet, than he loves
her; they no sooner meet, than they want to be married; they are
no sooner married, than they propose to die rather than be
separated. Their haste and practicality is another, younger generation's version of the haste and practicality of Capulet when he
demands his daughter's obedience:

> Hang thee, young baggage, disobedient wretch!
> I tell thee what: get thee to church o'Thursday,
> Or never after look me in the face.
> Speak not, reply not, do not answer me!
> My fingers itch.
>
>   (III. v. 160–4)

Absolute obedience to a parent, like obedience to a monarch, is
a concept that Shakespeare questions in these plays. He must
have been aware of the contemporary debates on parenting and
on the pamphlets circulating offering contrasting views on the
duty of children to follow their parent's wishes in such matters
as choice of partner. Louis Wright, in his study of the middle
class in Elizabethan England,[7] cites two contrasting pamphlets
that appeared in 1589 and 1591 respectively: John Stockwood's *A
Bartholomew Fairing for Parentes . . . Shewing that children are not to
marie, without the consent of their parentes, in whose power and choise
it lieth to provide wives and husbands for their sonnes and daughters,*
which insisted on the absolute authority of parents, and Charles
Gibbon's *A Work worth the Reading. Wherein is contayned, ffive
profitable and pithy Questions, very expedient, as well for Parents to*

perceive howe to bestowe their Children in marriage, and to dispose their
goods at their death: as for all other Persons to receive great profit by
the rest of the matters herein expressed, which took a more liberal
line and argued that many social evils were caused by forced
marriages.

Rebellion against parental authority is primarily against the
father. The mother is absent in *A Midsummer Night's Dream*, and
likewise in *Henry IV, Part 1*. In *Romeo and Juliet* there are two
mother figures, the Nurse and Lady Capulet, but both have no
power and both urge Juliet to compromise and obey her father.
The powerlessness of mothers is stated right at the start of the
play, when Capulet and Montague try to intervene in the brawl
and their wives seek to hold them back. Later, when Juliet is
found on her bed presumed dead, her mother's grief is for the
loss of a child, whilst her father's grief is couched in terms of loss
of inheritance.

In all three plays a subtle point is made about the authority of
the father. That the father must be obeyed is clear; the forces of
law are on his side. But in every case the father is proved wrong
by the events that take place. Capulet tries to force his daughter
to marry against her will, and her disobedience triggers the
eventual catastrophe. Moreover, his insistence on the feud with
the Montagues is shown to be not only foolish but against the
forces of life itself. When the Capulet parents see their daughter's body, Capulet can still only think in terms of the feud:

> O heavens! O wife, look how our daughter bleeds!
> This dagger hath mista'en, for lo his house
> Is empty on the back of Montague,
> And it mis-sheathed in my daughter's bosom!
>
> (V. iii. 202–5)

With their children dead, their wives dead or dying from grief,
Capulet and Montague finally agree to end the feud, though the
terms in which they make their peace are purely commercial and
the best that they can offer are statues of Romeo and Juliet made
of gold. That Shakespeare wanted to stress the vulgarity of the
two fathers and depict them in a less than sympathetic light is
borne out by comparison with his source text, Arthur Brooke's

The Tragicall Historye of Romeus and Juliet (1562), which does not mention the death of the wives, nor the golden statues.

The wishes of the father in *A Midsummer Night's Dream* are overruled by Theseus, when he has found the lovers asleep and heard their stories. Egeus still tries to demand the power of the law, but the couples have settled the problem themselves and natural law, that is love, holds sway. Such a development in the plot is in keeping with the purpose of the play, which critics agree was written for the celebration of a marriage, possibly that of Elizabeth Vere and William, Earl of Derby in January 1595 or that of Elizabeth Carey and Thomas Berkeley in February 1596, both brides being god-daughters of Queen Elizabeth. Nevertheless, the Pyramus and Thisbe play-within-the-play provides a warning of the tragic consequences of disobedience. What brings about the eventual harmony in *A Midsummer Night's Dream* is a combination of magic and new, more humane paternal powers, embodied in the figures of Oberon and Theseus.

King Henry, in *Henry IV, Part 1*, is also shown to be in the wrong, but in this play the process is more complex. Henry wishes his son had been exchanged at birth for Northumberland's son; by the end of the play Hotspur is dead, killed by the Prince who has proved to be the worthiest champion of the two. Effectively, Prince Henry and Hotspur are two aspects of the son archetype, while King Henry and Falstaff are two aspects of the father. Hotspur and Falstaff are most immediately sympathetic, but both are flawed characters and exposed as inadequate models to follow. Hotspur, says King Henry, is 'the theme of honour's tongue' (I. i. 80), a great warrior famous for his bravery, whilst Henry wastes his time in taverns. Yet when the Prince, in a tavern speech, mocks Hotspur's military prowess, he also pinpoints his fatal flaw:

> I am not yet of Percy's mind, the Hotspur of the north, he that kills me some six or seven dozen of Scots at a breakfast, washes his hands, and says to his wife, 'Fie upon this quiet life, I want work.' (II. iv. 100–3)

Hotspur does not pause to reflect, he rushes headlong into everything. King Henry sees the soldier in him, but does not see the rebel at first, but with his own son, he sees nothing but a

wastrel, failing to recognise a potential king. Only when Henry
beats Douglas, and so saves King Henry's life, is the king
reconciled to the son he has failed to understand:

> KING: Stay and breathe a while.
>   Thou hast redeemed thy lost opinion,
>   And showed thou makest some tender of my life
>   In this fair rescue thou hast brought to me.
> PRINCE: O God, they did me too much injury
>   That ever said I hearkened for your death.
>
> (V. iv. 46–51)

The absolute power of fathers is challenged in all three plays,
and in all three, fathers make errors of judgement. But although
twentieth-century directors of film and theatre, together with
some teachers, have sought to make these plays accessible by
stressing their relevance to contemporary teenagers at odds with
their parents, this grossly oversimplifies matters. The younger
generation is not straightforwardly heroic or admirable in
contrast to narrow-minded elders. Each generation has its faults
and the younger characters display a tendency to exaggeration
and an unrealistic attitude to the constraints of time.

The four lovers of *A Midsummer Night's Dream* are singularly
vapid and silly, as their exaggerated languages indicates. To take
just one example, Hippolyta's verdict of the Mechanical's play is
that it is 'the silliest stuff that ever I heard', a remark triggered
by the recitation of speeches such as Thisbe's:

> O wall! Full often hast thou heard my moans,
> For parting my fair Pyramus and me.
> My cherry lips have often kissed thy stones;
> Thy stones with hair and lime knit up in thee.
>
> (V. i. 187–90)

If we compare this with the speech uttered by Demetrius when
he wakes after the love potion has been administered and sees
Helena, the difference is negligible:

> O Helen, goddess, nymph, perfect, divine!
> To what, my love, shall I compare thine eyne?

Crystal is muddy. O, how ripe in show
Thy lips, those kissing cherries, tempting grow!
(III. ii. 136–40)

The lovers are depicted as foolish from the start, and Theseus's equation of lunatics, lovers and poets is very apt. Lovers are afflicted, they suffer from a form of madness that deprives them of reason, and they rush headlong into situations from which they cannot extricate themselves. Time for lovers becomes divorced from reality, and they wish time away in order to more quickly reach their goal. The play actually opens with Theseus counting the days and nights to his wedding, yet the action takes place in a single night. Hippolyta, wiser than her future husband, reminds him of the gap between real time and lovers' time:

Four days will quickly steep themselves in night:
Four nights will quickly dream away the time.
(I. i. 7–8)

Likewise, in *Romeo and Juliet*, the lovers' action is headlong. They rush into each other's arms, and in one of the most powerful speeches of the whole play, Juliet calls upon the chariot of the sun to rush down into the west and bring night and her longed-for Romeo ('Gallop apace, you fiery-footed steeds – III. ii 1). Friar Lawrence continually advises patience and restraint, but his advice is not heeded. Living at high speed, real time is meaningless to them. When the messenger who is sent to Romeo after his banishment cannot get through because of plague in the neighbouring city, Friar Lawrence's attempt to bring the lovers together ends in disaster. Romeo cannot wait, he hears of Juliet's suppose death and rushes back to Verona. Like the lovers in *A Midsummer Night's Dream*, Romeo and Juliet are also touched with madness.

In *Henry IV, Part 1*, the undesirability of precipitate action is clearly exemplified in Hotspur. Henry, like Hamlet, bides his time, while Hotspur rushes into combat. When Hotspur comes face to face with Henry in battle, the symbolic aspect of the struggle between the two men is made explicit: Henry represents the more calculating, reasoning aspect of kingship, while Hotspur is more glamorous but ultimately less sound. We are left in

no doubt as to which has the more desirable personality for a
future ruler:

> HOTSPUR: If I mistake not, thou are Harry Monmouth.
> PRINCE: Thou speakest as if I would deny my name.
> HOTSPUR: My name is Harry Percy.
> PRINCE: Why then I see
> A very valiant rebel of the name.
> I am the Prince of Wales, and think not, Percy,
> To share with me in glory any more.
> Two stars keep not their motion in one sphere,
> Nor can one England brook a double reign
> Of Harry Percy and the Prince of Wales.
>
> (V. iv. 58–66)

There can only be one successor to the throne; Henry's *alter ego*
must be destroyed. Likewise, a son can only have one father, and
so as the reconciliation between King Henry and son son takes
place, the marginalisation of Falstaff is assured.

All three plays conclude with statements about order. When
King Henry and his son have come together, they prepare to
make a united stand against rebel forces. 'Rebellion in this land
shall lose his sway', prophesies the king, preparing to go to
Wales to fight the rebel Glendower. It has sometimes been
suggested that because the play ends with the prospect of further
war, rather than with peace, that this signifies a lack of resolution
on Shakespeare's part, but this interpretation is unlikely. This
was the first play in a chronological sequence of three, and the
ending is appropriate in that it resolves the preceding action and
opens the way for further developments, a device that we find
entirely acceptable with television series today. What is
important in *Henry IV, Part 1* is the way in which father and son
come to terms with the rebellion of the one and the dis-
appointment of the other. Their domestic crisis is played out
against a crisis on a national scale, armed rebellion against the
throne.

A Midsummer Night's Dream concludes with a blessing and a
fairy song, a fitting conclusion to a wedding entertainment,
though even here there are reminders of fearful things – of
deformed children, 'the blots of Nature's hand', and the graves

that gape to let forth their spirits. Puck's epilogue brings in once again the image of the venemous serpent. The implications of the conclusion are clear: order has been restored, the disruption caused by the overturning of natural order is now over, but life is not a dream, it is full of dark corners that can be faced, even though not illuminated, by love.

The concluding speech of *Romeo and Juliet* is spoken by the prince, who has insisted, despite the passion for vengeance of the parents, on holding a full enquiry to find out what has happened. Theseus, the equivalent authority figure in *A Midsummer Night's Dream*, simply takes at face value the incoherent ramblings of Lysander and Demetrius and proceeds to overrule Egeus, doubtless out of a sense of lover's solidarity. The prince, however, demands not only to hear accounts of what has happened but also to see the evidence. When he has heard enough, he summarises the situation and draws conclusions about the feud between the Montagues and the Capulets:

> Where be these enemies? Capulet, Montague?
> See what a scourge is laid upon your hate,
> That heaven finds means to kill your joys with love!
> And I for winking at your discords too
> Have lost a brace of kinsmen. All are punished.
>
> (V. iii. 291–5)

The prince acknowledges his own lack of authority in these lines, for despite his threats in the opening scene of the play, the fighting has continued and there have been more deaths. The responsibility of the ruler for the continuance of a state of civil disobedience is made very plain, and was to reappear elsewhere in Shakespeare's work. The breakdown of the relationship between parents and children in the domestic arena is paralleled by the breakdown of the relationship between ruler and subjects.

The convention of considering Shakespeare's Elizabethan plays as tragedies, comedies or histories is a restrictive one, for it can mean that similarities are easily overlooked. In fact, divisions are not clearcut at all, as can be seen in the case of the three plays under consideration here, where there are strong thematic parallels. All three plays explore the relationship between parents (particularly fathers) and children, and through that private relationship the plays also explore the wider, public relationship between individual and ruler and question the basis of patriarchal law.

Romeo and Juliet was probably written in 1594–5, and *A Midsummer Night's Dream* dates from the same period, being written either before or after *Romeo and Juliet*. *Henry IV, Part 1* was written slightly later, probably in 1597–8 and consequently shares fewer immediate stylistic features with the other two plays. Nevertheless, the link between all three is clearly the emphasis on the breakdown of family allegiances, and the misunderstanding between the generations. Shakespeare's manipulation of his source material shows the ways in which he sought to draw attemtion to that central concern.

A Midsummer Night's Dream is unusual in that there is no clear source, and its length (it is the fourth shortest play by Shakespeare) suggests that it was written for a special occasion, for a private performance at a marriage ceremony. There are various literary sources that have been traced in the play, but as has been indicated above (and discussed at length by Jan Kott), considering that he was writing for a wedding, Shakespeare has not created a world of lyricism and lightness, and his comic vision has dark undertones. This darkness is linked to the fundamental issues of authority in crisis (the fair king and queen at war with one another, the daughter rejecting her father's proposed bridegroom) and so we are reminded that even in an occasional piece such as this, Shakespeare was still working with problematic material. *A Midsummer Night's Dream* may be a comedy, but it is also a very political play.

The reworking of Brooke's poem in *Romeo and Juliet* also shows how Shakespeare shaped his material to focus attention on significant issues. The story of the doomed lovers is archetypal, but the setting of their story within the context of warring families in a Renaissance city-state politicises the issues, and Shakespeare's handling of Brooke politicises the issues still further. Brooke's poem is a more linear tragedy, with the emphasis on the lovers who are caught up in the family feud; Shakespeare's play opens with the fight between rival factions and ends with the prince regretting his own lack of willpower and our attention is therefore directed to the public context in which the lovers are located.

Henry IV, Part 1 derives obviously from Holinshed's *Chronicles of England* (1587), but Shakespeare reworked the account of Hotspur and created the figure of Falstaff who, as has often been discussed, was based on a real person, Sir John Oldcastle, a knight and companion of Henry V who was eventually burned at the stake for heresy. By creating a second son-figure and a second father-figure, Shakespeare underlines the central theme of the play, that painful process whereby a man learns to become both a good son and a good prince, a process paralleled by the father's recognition that his own opinion of his son may be inadequate. King Henry is as out of touch with his son Henry as the prince is with his subjects, as Capulet, Montague and Egeus are with the generation to which their children belong. In short, they are personifications of authority in decay and the younger generation, in rebelling against their parents, does not seek anarchy, but rather seeks to assert a new system of values, firmly rooted in a wider, more humanitarian vision of the world. Although never explicit or, indeed, even hinted at within the plays, the image of an ageing, childless monarch presiding over an impatient much younger court must have come to the mind of more than one member of the Elizabethan audiences who first saw the plays performed. Today, the clash between generations strikes a different note, but is nevertheless of such significance in contemporary societies that these three plays are amongst the most frequently performed of all Shakespeare's work.

5
The Boundaries of Comedy:
The Taming of the Shrew and
The Merchant of Venice

The popularity of Shakespeare's early history plays established him firmly in the public eye, so much so that in Greene's famous attack of 1592 he is described as 'the only shake-scene in the country', the man 'as well able to bombast out a blank verse as the best of you'. Greene died before he was able to see the upstart crow, as he so rudely termed Shakespeare, begin to acquire success in another theatrical form, one that has perhaps found even greater success with subsequent generations of audiences: comedy.

Shakespeare's earliest comedies are *The Comedy of Errors*, *The Taming of the Shrew* and *Two Gentlemen of Verona*, though the sequence of the writing of these three plays is arguable. Of the three, it is *The Taming of the Shrew* that is the best known today, and *Two Gentlemen of Verona* is generally regarded as one of the more obscure plays in the Shakespeare canon. There is no record of a performance of the play until 1762 in a revised version, and although we can assume that it must have been performed early in the 1590s, the absence of information suggests that it was not a great success in its own time either.

These three early comedies are very different from one another in both structure and subject matter, and many critics have suggested that they should be considered as examples of Shakespeare's apprenticeship in comedy. *Two Gentlemen of Verona* is essentially a romantic comedy, dealing with the traditional story of two good friends who both fall in love with the same woman and, as has often been pointed out, there are a great many features of the play that prefigure later developments in works such as *The Merchant of Venice, A Midsummer Night's Dream, As You Like It* or *Twelfth Night.* The lovers – Proteus, Valentine, Julia and Silvia – are quite unmemorable, and the figure who is most prominent in the play is the clown Launce, who may well have been added later, once Shakespeare began to work closely with Will Kemp.[1] The role of Launce is curiously unintegrated in the play, and his first appearance in act II is a solo comedian's *tour de force.* Accompanied by his dog Crab, Launce talks directly to the audience, his patter in the form of a monologue that could fit into virtually any play or even stand completely alone, as this example demonstrates:

> I think Crab, my dog, be the sourest-natured dog that lives. My mother weeping, my father wailing, my sister crying, our maid howling, our cat wringing her hands, and all our house in great perplexity, yet did not this cruel-hearted cur shed one tear. He is a stone, a very pebblestone, and no more pity in him than a dog. A Jew would have wept to see our parting. Why, my grandam, having no eyes, look you, wept herself blind at my parting. Nay, I'll show you the manner of it.
>
> (II. iii. 5–14)

This speech is the stuff of the stand-up comic, and a variant on it still continues today in television advertisements for example, where the lugubrious dog acts as a foil for his soliloquising master in an attempt to sell a particular product. What we seem to have with *The Two Gentlemen of Verona*, therefore, is a play that contains a superb part for a gifted comedian that is loosely linked to the main narrative line of thwarted love, betrayal, disguise and mistaken identity through the device of having Launce serve Proteus. Launce, like his companion Speed, are both described as 'clownish servants' to Proteus and Valentine respectively, and this dual relationship recalls that of the masters and servants in another comedy from roughly the same time, *The Comedy of Errors*.

The sources for *The Two Gentlemen of Verona* include Brooke's poem that provided the basis for *Romeo and Juliet*, a romance by Jorge de Montemayor and works by John Lyly, though the story of friendship that is put at risk by passion can be said to be archetypal and was certainly enormously popular throughout medieval and Renaissance Europe. In contrast to these varied sources, *The Comedy of Errors* derives from Plautus, though the fact that Plautus's *Menaechmi* did not appear in English translation until 1595, after the appearance of Shakespeare's play, has led to speculation that Shakespeare may have seen a manuscript version or may even have had enough Latin to be able to adapt the original. Whatever the background to the play, as the editors of the Oxford Edition of Shakespeare agree, *The Comedy of Errors* is his most classically constructed play, 'a kind of diploma piece, as if Shakespeare were displaying his ability to outshine both his classical progenitors and their English imitators'.[2]

To his Latin source tale of mistaken identity and confusion Shakespeare added a second dimension of comic misunderstanding: besides the twin brothers, separated since childhood, he adds twin servants who have likewise been separated. All is revealed at the end, when the Abbess turns out to be mother of the two Antipholuses, and the four boys, two masters and two servants, separated by a shipwreck, are restored to one another. Coleridge declares this Shakespearean addition of the two Dromios to be a sign that the play may be more properly categorised as a farce than as a comedy:

A proper farce is mainly distinguished from comedy by the license allowed, and even required, in the fable, in order to produce strange and laughable situations. The story need not be probable, it is enough that it is possible. A comedy would scarcely allow even the two Antipholuses . . . but farce dares add two Dromios, and is justified in so doing by the laws of its end and constitution. In a word, farces commence in a postulate, which must be granted.[3]

The ludicrous adventures of the two sets of twins who finally come together without at first realising is obviously strong comic material. The play moves at a fast pace and there is a great deal of physical comic business besides wordplay. But as in all Shakespeare's comedies (and increasingly so in the later works) there are darker elements. The separation of the children from their mother and of the Abbess from her husband is potentially tragic, as is the threatened death of Aegeon. In V. i Aegeon's distraught speech to Antipholus of Ephesus prefigures the desperation of Lear and Gloucester, both fathers confronted with the horror of filial rejection. Moreover, besides the comedy of misrepresentation and mistaken identity is another darkly comic line, one that is more controversial and potentially problematic: the stormy marriage of the philandering Antipholus of Ephesus and his jealous wife Adriana.

It has often been noted that this marriage bears some similarities to the marriage of Katharina and Petruchio in *The Taming of the Shrew*. The difference, of course, is that Katharina is sharp-tongued before her marriage and her husband endeavours to bring her into line, whilst Adriana is jealous and unhappy because she feels neglected by her husband. Both plays utilise another comic archetype, that of the nagging wife, a character who still provides comedians with ready material today.

In her Introduction to the New Cambridge Edition of *The Taming of the Shrew*, Ann Thompson discusses the ways in which the play has been revised in accordance with the differing views of actors and producers and the different expectations of audiences:

> Thus throughout its stage history *The Taming of the Shrew* has probably received fewer straight performances than any other Shakespearean play of comparable popularity on the stage. The apparently unrelieved ethic of male supremacy has proved unpalatable, and generation after generation of producers and directors have altered and adapted the text in more or less flagrant ways in order to soften the ending. . . . Productions of the play have frequently attracted whatever thoughts were in the air on the perennially topical subjects of violence and sexual politics, and this tendency can hardly fail to increase in our own time.[4]

Ann Thompson is quite right to point out the difficulties pre-

sented by the ending, when in response to a bet among the men
as to whose wife is the most obedient, Katharina makes a speech
proclaiming her absolute subjugation to her husband's will:

> Thy husband is thy lord, thy life, thy keeper,
> Thy head, thy sovereign . . .
> Such duty as the subject owes the prince,
> Even such a woman oweth to her husband.
>   (V. ii. 146–7; 155–6)

Performers have variously interpreted this speech as: *ironic*,
Katharina has not changed at all and is mocking Petruchio and
the other women; *conspiratorial*, Katharina is now in love with
Petruchio and shares a secret joke with him in putting down the
other women and their partners; *bitter*, Katharina is subject to the
authority of her husband and has no choice but to do as he
demands.

In her splendid book of interviews with contemporary
Shakespearean actresses, Carol Rutter talks to Paola Dionisotti,
Sinead Cusack and Fiona Shaw, Katharinas in RSC productions,
respectively, in 1978 (directed by Michael Bogdanov), 1982
(directed by Barrie Kyle) and 1987 (directed by Jonathan Miller).
All three women discuss problematic aspects of the directors'
interpretations of the play and their own feminist readings, and
all three also draw attention to some of the difficulties inherent
in the text itself. Sinead Cusack's interpretation of the role is the
most optimistic, in that she sees the play as 'about Kate being
liberated', but the other two take a different view. Both point out
that Katharina, the supposed shrew, has very few lines and is
off-stage at crucial decision-making moments. Paola Dionisotti's
interpretation is a radical revision of the popular conception of
the play, exemplified in the Hollywood version that starred
Elizabeth Taylor:

> I wanted the play to be about Kate and about a woman
> instinctively fighting sexism. But I don't really think that's
> what the play is about. It's not the story of Kate: it's the story
> of Petruchio. He gets all the soliliquies, he gets the moments
> of change.[5]

This view of the play is reinforced by the fact that Petruchio is an outsider, a kind of soldier of fortune who comes to Padua to find himself a wife. He is quite explicit about his reasons for coming:

> Such wind as scatters young men through the world
> To seek their fortunes farther than at home
> Where small experience grows. But, in a few,
> Signor Hortensio, thus it stands with me:
> Antonio my father is deceased
> And I have thrust myself into this maze,
> Happily to wive and thrive as best I may. . . .
>   therefore, if thou know
> One rich enough to be Petruchio's wife –
> As wealth is burden of my wooing dance . . .
> I come to wive it wealthily in Padua;
> If wealthily, then happily in Padua.
>   (I. ii. 49–55; 65–7; 74–5)

Katharina, for her part, is shown as wanting to be married, and in II. i, when she attacks her sister, Bianca, she complains to her father that he prefers Bianca, giving as evidence the fact that he is taking more pains to marry his younger daughter:

> She is your treasure, she must have a husband.
> I must dance barefoot on her wedding day
> And, for your love to her, lead apes in hell.
>   (II. i. 32–4)

Katharina will lose status if her younger sister marries first, and she is depicted as bitter and angry about the prospect of becoming an old maid. But when, later in the same scene, Petruchio announces his intention of marrying her and her father thankfully agrees, Katharina has only one line – 'I'll see thee hanged on Sunday first' – which both men deliberately choose to ignore. The contract is sealed with a handshake in front of witnesses, like any proper commercial transaction, and the wedding date is fixed regardless of the bride's wishes. The speed with which the whole matter is settled recalls the speed of the decision taken by Capulet to see his daughter married to Tybalt.

The treatment of Katharina after marriage is brutal, but it is presented as farce and the pace of the action, which is interset with scenes of the wooing of Bianca, prevents us from focusing too intently on what in other circumstances would be exposed as cruelty. Petruchio, once a husband, has rights over his wife that give him absolute power. In his speech that is effectively a parody of the Old Testament definition of a wife, he states his position as owner of Katharina:

> I will be master of what is mine own.
> She is my goods, my chattels; she is my house,
> My household-stuff, my field, my barn,
> My horse, my ox, my ass, my anything,
> And here she stands.
>
> (III. ii. 229–33)

Unpleasant as it has been for subsequent generations of audiences to accept (and it is particularly distasteful for those of us who have benefited so much from the feminism of the past decades), it should be recognised that in the depiction of both Petruchio and Katharina there is little room for sentiment or sympathy. Katharina is both a shrew and a woman afraid of being left on the shelf, and as Lisa Jardine argues, hostility towards women who were seen to be unruly was widespread:

> Katharina (Kate) in *The Taming of the Shrew*, and Beatrice in *Much Ado About Nothing* strike the primitive fear of disorder and misrule into the hearts of men around them, although their witty dialogue seems to the modern audience charming and alert. . . . There is, of course, as critics point out, a heavy irony in the 'tamings' in these plays. But I think we are misled if we take that irony as some kind of benevolent approval for women's verbal licence.[6]

Louis Wright supports this view in his study of the Elizabethan middle classes, pointing out that the *sine qua non* of a stable bourgeois society was a stable domestic situation.[7] Unfaithfulness, shrewishness, slovenliness, extravagance, gossiping – all were condemned as destructive vices in women, symptomatic of wider disorder and disintegration. Wright notes that through the

English Renaissance, attention came to be increasingly directed towards the relationship between the sexes, as Protestant ideas of marriage took hold. He also draws attention to the proliferation of instructions for the maintenance of domestic harmony:

> From the first half of the sixteenth century onward, English writers on domestic themes busied themselves in the propagation of their notions about the best methods for maintaining the proper harmony between husband and wife in the government of the home. It is worth noting that most of these treatises were patently written from the middle-class point of view and express the ideals of the rising mercantile classes.[8]

Katharina, like Adriana, is so far from meeting that ideal that audiences were likely to have been totally unsympathetic, in much the same way as the other characters in both plays are unsympathetic to the complaints of the two women. The shrewish wife is the butt of jokes, and the audience colludes with the husband in seeing her brought to heel, in the same way as audiences (especially children) collude with Punch when he beats Judy to death after killing the baby.

Aristotle's notion of comedy is based on the view that comedy represents people as worse than they actually are. The ridiculous, he suggests, consists of some form of error or ugliness that is harmless – 'the comic mask is distorted and ugly, but causes no pain'.[9] Generations of critics approaching texts such as *The Taming of the Shrew* have sought to apply Aristotle's teaching, despite the apparent evidence to the contrary, and when they have failed to explain away the darkness at the heart of the play, they have, as Ann Thompson reminds us, kept quiet about it.[10] But Aristotle's view of comedy, which stands in a binary opposition to his concept of tragedy, was born out of a society at a particular moment in time, a slave-owning society which was structured on rigid hierarchical premises and, as we know very well, the object of laughter can also be the object of derision and loathing.

One of the most important twentieth-century plays about comedy is Trevor Griffiths's *Comedians*. Written in 1976, the play analyses the nature of humour and explores the question of the limits of the comic. His protagonist is a stand-up comedian who runs a course for other would-be artistes, and through the play we are shown how his students work off stereotypes, directing the jokes at marginalised members of society such as women, Jews or Asians, or at those who have low social status, such as members of the working class, old people, the handicapped or the mentally ill. In a scene that exposes the prejudices that lie behind the jokes his students are delivering, the old teacher explains:

It's not the jokes! It's what lies behind 'em. It's the attitude![11]

Griffiths demonstrates that the joke is by no means painless; rather, comedy can expose the brutal realities of prejudice and hatred that lie below the surface of supposedly civilised societies. He also shows something much more insidious: that the joker may not be aware of the ideological implications of the joke, and the fear and loathing may never be consciously recognised. The taming of Katharina, which is a process full of violence and savagery, reflects the position of women in Elizabethan society rather than any special misogyny on the part of Shakespeare. Paola Dionisotti is quite right when she says that the play is primarily about Petruchio; we follow his story, from his arrival in Padua to his winning of the wager, and throughout the play we are invited to be on his side, and rejoice with his success in obtaining both money and a properly respectful wife.

If *The Taming of the Shrew* presents twentieth-century audiences with a problem regarding its sexism, *The Merchant of Venice* presents us with a problem of similar, perhaps even more emotionally charged, dimensions. *The Merchant of Venice* has been more frequently performed than any of Shakespeare's plays with the exception of *Hamlet*, though it was not revived in England after 1605 until Granville's version, *The Jew of Venice*, in 1701. What the play offers is a rich, meaty part for a virtuoso actor, and Shylock has been played by actors such as Charles Macklin, Edmund Kean, Henry Irving and Laurence Olivier. However, as M. Mahood points out in his Introduction to the New Cambridge Edition of the play, the portrayal of the Jew has undergone a series of very different metamorphoses, ranging from the sympathetic to the outright hostile.[11] In the twentieth century, with first the pogroms in Eastern Europe and then the Holocaust of

Nazi Germany, portrayals of Shylock have been even more complicated:

> 'I am a Jew' now evoked an uneasiness which deepened as the harrassment of European Jews turned into persecution and finally into genocide. Whatever his interpretation of the role, the actor of Shylock had to take into account the distress and guilt of a whole generation of playgoers.[12]

The publisher of the 1600 edition summarised the main points of interest in the play as follows:

> The most excellent Historie of the Merchant of Venice. With the extreame crueltie of Shylocke the Jewe towards the sayd Merchant, in cutting a just pound of flesh: and the obtayning of Portia by the choyse of three chests. As it hath been divers times acted by the Lord Chamberlaine his Servants. Written by William Shakespeare.[13]

The stories of the three caskets and the pound of flesh that intersect through the play draw upon archetypal folk-tale images, and both are linked to the theme of commerce that lies at the heart of the play. Bassanio wins Portia by choosing the casket that has the least rich appearance, while Shylock loses his daughter and his revenge because he sets too much store by the accumulation of wealth. The moral point being made here is a simplistic one, but behind that simplicity what is actually being said about commerce and morality is more ambiguous. Bassanio may be the hero who wins the lady, but the terms on which he sets out to woo her remind us of Petruchio. Before remarking on her beauty and her virtues, Bassanio tells his friend that Portia is 'richly left'. Wealth in a wife is as important as virtue, and Jessica is careful to ensure that she takes her dowry with her when she elopes from Shylock's house also.

It has often been pointed out that the alternative title of the play was *The Jew of Venice*, and certainly the character of Shylock, is much more challenging for an actor than that of the merchant himself, Antonio. Shylock does not appear until the third scene of the play, and when he enters he is midway through a business transaction with Bassanio. This interest in practicalities stands in

sharp contrast to the opening of the previous two scenes, the first
with a speech by Antonio on his inexplicable sense of world-
weariness, 'In sooth I know not why I am so sad./It wearies me,
you say it wearies you' and the second with Portia complaining
to Nerissa that her 'little body is aweary of this great world'. This
sense of melancholy pervades the play, and even the clown is not
immune from it. Like Launce in *The Two Gentlemen of Verona*,
Launcelot Gobbo enters with a monologue, but in contrast to the
comedian's routine with a dog, Launcelot Gobbo wrestles with
his conscience. He is trying to decide whether to run away from
his master Shylock, and argues his way towards liberty through
a circuitous, almost Jesuitical route:

> To be ruled by my conscience, I should stay with the Jew my
> master who – God bless the mark! – is a kind of devil; and to
> run away from the Jew, I should be ruled by the fiend who –
> saving your reverence – is the devil himself. Certainly the Jew
> is the very devil incarnation, and, in my conscience, my
> conscience is but a kind of hard conscience to offer to counsel
> me to stay with the Jew. The fiend gives the more friendly
> counsel: I will run, fiend, my heels are at your commandment,
> I will run. (II. ii. 16–24)

Launcelot's contempt for the Jew, his master, recalls the patter of
Launce, who has a repertoire of jokes about Jews. The figure of
the clown in both plays is therefore associated with anti-
Jewishness, and what we seem to be confronted with here is the
troubling evidence of popular anti-Semitism in Elizabethan
England embodied in the figure of the servant, the most obvious
man of the people, in contrast to the bourgeois merchant class of
his masters.
   The famous 'Hath not a Jew eyes?' speech, in which Shylock
pleads for the humanity of the despised race is certainly very
powerful but is immediately undercut by the ensuing dialogue
with Tubal. Shylock has just argued that he is as capable of
feeling as any Christian; now the news of his daughter's
elopement with his jewels produces the blackly comic 'I would
my daughter were dead at my foot, and the jewels in her ear.'
He has just asked 'If you prick us, do we not bleed?'; now when

he hears how much Jessica spent in one night in Genoa he uses the image of the knife very differently:

> SHYLOCK: Thou stick'st a dagger in me; I shall never see my gold again. Four score ducats at a sitting! Four score ducats!
> TUBAL: There came divers of Antonio's creditors in my company to Venice that swear he cannot choose but break.
> SHULOCK: I am very glad of it. I'll plague him, I'll torture him. I am glad of it.
>
> (III. i. 106–14)

There is no humanity here, this is the language of the archetypal comic villain, the monster we all love to hate. That the monster is Jewish is, alas, an aspect of Elizabethan society that is as distressing to contemporary minds as was the public execution or mutilation, the baiting of live birds and animals and the enthusiastic support of the newly developing slave trade, all equally accepted features of the 1590s. The execution of in 1594 Ruy Lopez, a Portuguese Jew accused of trying to poison the queen, led to a surge of anti-Semitism, including the revival of Marlowe's grotesque play, *The Jew of Malta*.

Written in 1910, Ortega y Gasset's essay on Shylock reminds us of the horrors of anti-Semitism:

> The miserable howls of the Venetian Jew direct our attention to one of the worst evils of history: anti-Semitism.
> Such a passion is not a fleeting one; Shylock is not an anecdote extracted from a frivolous Italian centon. . . . The other races have let fall on the Jews, drop by drop, all the might of their hatred. Jews have been ill-treated, scorned and exploited a thousand times. . . . When a medieval Christian wanted to praise God in a very special way, he would kill Jews.[14]

As a Spaniard, a citizen of the country who expelled, butchered or forcibly converted its entire Jewish population within living memory of some contemporaries of Shakespeare, Ortega y Gasset was well placed to express the view that Shylock is an archetypal figure. In the *Jew of Venice*, 'Shakespeare conjures up a millenial pain', but that pain is swamped by the anti-Semitic sentiments of the other characters in the play.

Thomas Moison, in a recent essay on *The Merchant of Venice*, seeks to answer the important question of exactly what a contemporary Elizabethan audience would have found in the play.[15] He suggests that among aspects which we might find less apparent is a double-sided statement about usury – on the one hand Shylock is a usurer and the loathing in which such men were held is well documented, but on the other hand Bassanio and Antonio are guilty of profligacy and a certain arrogant irresponsibility. Shylock stands to be revenged not because he made the pact with Antonio in the first place, but because Antonio entered into it recklessly. In a society where overseas trade was beginning to develop as the lifeline for a depressed economy, such irresponsible behaviour was hardly conducive to future success. The world-weariness that Antonio feels is a sign that he is a man not altogether comfortable with his fellow members of the trading class. In response to Gratiano, who urges him to be less melancholy, Antonio replies with the famous lines:

> I hold the world but as the world, Gratiano:
> A stage where every man must play a part,
> And mine a sad one.
>
> (I. i. 77–9)

Significantly, Gratiano, who tries so hard to cheer Antonio up ('Let me play the Fool/With mirth and laughter let old wrinkles come') turns out to be the most vicious of the Jew-baiters, mocking Shylock in his downfall when it becomes clear that he will never get his pound of flesh and opposing even the forcible conversion that the Duke imposes upon the ruined Jew:

> In christening shalt thou have two godfathers:
> Had I been judge, thou shouldst have had ten more,
> To bring thee to the gallows, not the font.
>
> (IV. i. 398–400)

Gratiano the mirth-maker is also Gratiano the Jew-hater; we are reminded of figures such as Drake, Hawkins and Hakluyt, seafaring entrepreneurs, with singers and players in their cabins for shipboard entertainments and slaves in the hold, justifying their buccanneering and brutality not only because of the riches it would bring to them personally, but rather on account of the glory to the State and the 'salvation of many thousand soules, which the common enemie of mankind still detayneth in ignorance'.[16] Gratiano is untroubled by the melancholy (finer feelings?) displayed by Antonio. He is the man who knows how to seize opportunities when they present themselves. No sooner does Bassanio win Portia, than Gratiano announces his intention to marry Nerissa, and he greets Salario shortly afterwards with the statement that 'We are the Jasons, we have won the fleece' (III. ii. 240). If anyone is the stereotype of the successful entrepreneur in this play, it is Gratiano, and it is he who concludes the play with a suggestive speech about going to bed with Nerissa.

Discussing Shakespeare's ethics, Germaine Greer also reminds us of the gap between Elizabethan thinking and our own:

> Shakespeare does not provide us with a map of an ethical system. It would be futile to attempt to extrapolate from his works any collection of ethical imperatives, if for no other reason than that he shared with his contemporaries a profound and vivid sense of morality as something organic and dynamic, which was not given to any individual to understand in its entirety. The playwright's task was not to expound it, but to convey a lively and unforgettable impression of its reality.[17]

This is a very apt statement, and it helps to resolve the debate about Shakespeare's moral and political stance: was he a misogynist, an anti-Semite, an arch-conservative, a man whose views would not have been out of place within fascistic national socialist movements today, or was he instead a liberal humanist, pro-Jewish, pro-women, pro-Moors? Even to pose such questions in these terms is absurd. Shakespeare was simply a product of his own age, and furthermore he was a man of the theatre, in the business of bringing in audiences, raising funds and keeping on the right side of his patrons, like anyone else in any other culture who works in the commercial entertainment business. There is no doubt that the issues raised in plays like *The Merchant of Venice*, *The Comedy of Errors* and *The Taming of the Shrew* would have struck a chord in the minds of Elizabethan audiences, and there is also no doubt that we, in the late twentieth century, cannot approach these plays without an awareness of our own socio-historical context, which means that wife-beating, anti-Semitism and marriages of convenience are offensive, whether written in Shakespearean English or not.

What links us today with Shakespeare's time is the way in which these plays explore aspects of the comic that are painful and unpleasant. Behind the laughter, there is something else, and as we encounter the boundaries of comedy we are led to examine ourselves and to ask not only what are we laughing at, but what that laughter might conceal.

6
England, the World's Best Garden: *Henry IV, Part 2* and *Henry V*

In contrast to the seven editions of *Henry IV, Part 1* before 1623 (the date of publication of Shakespeare's plays in the Folio), there was only one printing of *Henry IV, Part 2*. In his Introduction to the New Penguin Edition of the play, Peter Davison draws this fact to our attention as an indicator of the difference in popularity of the two plays, though he adds that in his view *Part 2* is 'the more interesting and, in some ways, the greater play'.[1]

There has been a considerable amount of debate on the relationship between the two parts of *Henry IV* – whether the plays were devised together as two parts of a whole, or whether *Part 2* was written in the wake of the success of *Part 1*. Central to the debate, however, is the great difference between the two plays as regards characterisation, narrative development, mood and tone. *Part 1* is constructed around binary oppositions, with two images of an ideal princely son and two images of a father. *Part 2* is more complex and the focus of the play is not so clearly delineated. Falstaff appears early in the play, in I. ii, but he is older, more obviously afflicted with disease ('A pox of this gout! Or a gout of this pox!' – 1. 246) and there is greater malice in his dealings with the Lord Chief Justice than was apparent in any of his relationships in *Part 1*. Prince Henry does not appear until II. ii and his opening line reflects the overall mood of the play – 'Before God, I am exceeding weary' (l. 1).

The tendency, especially in recent years, to stage the two parts of *Henry IV* along with *Henry V* as a trilogy with one actor as the prince throughout, serves to play down the differences between the plays, rather than to expose them. If these plays are seen as a trilogy, the central character becomes Prince Henry, and the central theme becomes the way in which the young prince is educated to become a worthy successor to his father and an heroic English king. The profligate young man of *Part 1*, playing jokes on Falstaff and drinking in taverns is eventually transformed into the hero King Henry V, who leads the English to victory at Agincourt and is described by the Chorus in the Epilogue as 'this star of England', the man whose sword created the nation known as the world's best garden. But seeing the plays as a trilogy presents other difficulties if, as is commonly the case, directors also look for development of character in terms of psychological realism.

Character inconsistency in Shakespeare is notorious. The famous clichéd question that asks how many children did Lady Macbeth have offers a fine example of that inconsistency. Lady Macbeth tells us she has given suck and knows what it is to hold a child to her breast. But nowhere in the play is there any reference to Macbeth and his wife having children, and in fact the great difference between Macbeth and Banquo, Macduff and Duncan is that the last three have sons. Macbeth kills Macduff's children and tries to kill Banquo's and Duncan's, but he fails and, as the witches predict, the descendants of his enemy inherit his stolen kingdom. What then are we to conclude from Lady Macbeth's remark? That she had children and they died? And if so, does this go some way towards explaining why Macbeth and his Lady are so desperate for power, because they know they have no descendants? And if she were pregnant once, why not again? Or is she too old? In which case, how old might Macbeth and his wife be? The questions proliferate, and if we follow the line of psychological realism and consistency in characterisation, then Lady Macbeth offers either an insoluble puzzle or at best a study in neurosis or gynaecological complications.

Moreover, the method of analysing character as derived from

Stanislawski is by no means objective. In his notes on the staging
of *Othello*, which traces in detail the way in which he worked on
a Shakespeare play, Stanislawski confesses to feeling irritated
with Desdemona when she pleads with Othello on behalf of
Cassio. The psychological realism at play here is that of the male
chauvinist who does not like a woman to step out of place:

> I dislike Desdemona's constant pestering of Othello to forgive
> Cassio, as the play shows it. I think Desdemona is always
> doing it at the wrong moment. It becomes particularly
> obvious when the actor playing Othello throws passion and
> jealousy about all through his part. The result is that the
> spectator, seeing the husband in a bad mood, asks himself:
> Why does she bother him just now, couldn't she find a more
> opportune moment? Placing myself in the actress's position I
> feel it necessary to excuse this awkwardness. How do I go
> about it?[2]

The inconsistencies of characterisation in Shakespeare are
legion, as are inconsistencies in plot-line, in time spans, in
sequence of action. Critics have sought to explain away these
inconsistencies with all kinds of ingenious suggestions, but it
would be more helpful if we could seek to move back beyond
psychological realism as we understand it today and try to
imagine what it may have signified in Elizabethan England. This
is not to deny the power of Shakespeare's characters, or to
suggest that there is anything wrong with his writing, but rather
to assume that what we might see as inconsistency was not
always perceived as such. Lady Macbeth's speech draws upon
the powerful imagery of the demonic mother, willing to smash
her baby's skull rather than break an oath. The complex narrative
threads of Renaissance epic poems, for example, could be
dropped and taken up again by writer and reader alike, in ways
that contemporary readers find extremely difficult to deal with.
Likewise, in theatre, although his characters are created as roun-
ded beings, offering actors great opportunities for demonstrating
their performance skills, Shakespeare was a man of his time and
so gave little attention to tying up loose ends of plot and

character. What counted primarily was whether something or someone worked on a stage when an audience was present.

It is therefore not surprising to find little consistency of characterisation across three very different plays, which, although written roughly across a two-year period, between 1597 and 1599, are quite distinct from one another. The Henry of *Henry V* is quite different from the Henry of the two parts of *Henry IV*, which in turn differ from each other, nor can there really be said to be any logical progression other than on the purely thematic level. All these plays deal with the same historical personage and derive from a combination of Holinshed's *Chronicles* and the anonymous play of *c.* 1594 entitled *The Famous Victories of Henry the Fifth*, but beyond that there is no common thread.

Not only is the characterisation widely at variance between these three plays, but so also is the structure. *Henry IV, Part 2* opens with a speech by Rumour, 'painted full of tongues' and therefore takes on the quality of a pageant from the very start. There is also an epilogue, possibly spoken by William Kemp, the clown, promising a continuation to the story of Falstaff, though in fact in *Henry V*, Falstaff does not appear and what we have instead is an account of his death. In *Henry V* the device of the third-person narrator is used even more extensively, and the Chorus not only opens and closes the play, but introduces the other four acts as well. The foregrounding of this narrative element suggests that we are being invited to see the plays in some particular way, that our attention is being directed towards certain elements and probably away from attention on individuals.

In his Introduction to his collection of twentieth-century essays on *Henry IV, Part 2*, David Young draws attention to the circumstances surrounding the writing of the play:

> It is usually thought to be the sixteenth play in Shakespeare's canon. Thus it comes about midway in his total oeuvre and belongs, most certainly, to his artistic maturity. . . . It belongs to the late 1590s and thus to what is probably the richest decade (1595–1605) in the history of the English theatre, as well as to that part of Shakespeare's career in which he seems to have enjoyed his fullest success as a dramatist.[3]

Nevertheless, despite these apparently favourable circumstances there is a distinct sense of melancholy in the play, and L. C. Knights draws parallels with the darkening mood of the *Sonnets*.[4] The play is full of references to autumn and is dominated by old men. 'We are all diseased', says the Archbishop of York, reminding us of the previous king, deposed by Henry IV – 'of which disease/Our late King Richard being infected died' (IV. ii. 54; 57–8), while Doll Tearsheet reminds Falstaff of his mortality when she asks him rhetorically:

> Thou whoreson little tidy Bartholomew boar-pig, when wilt thou leave fighting a-days, and foining a-nights and begin to patch up thine old body for heaven? (II. iv. 235–7)

The play opens with a question, posed by the figure of Rumour, a reminder of the morality tradition that has often been suggested forms the basis of Shakespeare's creation of Falstaff. Rumour declares himself to be at home in the theatre, 'among my household', and asserts his supremacy in all times and all places. '[W]hich of you', he demands, 'will stop/The vent of hearing when loud Rumour speaks?' The power of Rumour is unassailable, and having established this he goes on to state his immediate function, which is to bring confused reports of success to the rebels opposed to the king. The first scene shows this process in operation, and as in traditional folk mythology, where everything happens in threes, we are given three versions of the outcome of the battle of Shrewsbury: first Lord Bardolph arrives with news of victory, then Travers arrives with more ambiguous news, and finally Morton arrives with an account of Hotspur's death and the king's victory.

From Rumour, then, the play moves straightaway into the rebel stronghold, but by showing us Northumberland's grief on hearing of his son's death, the rebels already win a certain amount of sympathy. This reversal of 'right' ways of thinking is continued in I. ii, where Falstaff, the old comic favourite from *Part 1* is introduced. The problem here is that Falstaff is different from the fat, mischievous knight that audiences had come to know and love; he enters asking his page about the results of a medical examination:

FALSTAFF: Sirrah, you giant, what says the doctor to my water?

PAGE: He said, sir, the water itself was a good, healthy water; but, for the party that owned it, he might have more diseases than he knew for.

(I. ii. 1–5)

If I. i introduces death, then I. ii introduces the motif of disease and decay that will run throughout the play, present in the language and made explicit through the physical appearance of a whole series of characters including Falstaff himself, the old 'forked radish' Justice Shallow, the three useless recruits, Wart, Feeble and Bullcalf, with his 'whoreson cold', Bardolph with his boils and pustules and the dying king, 'so thin that life looks through and will break out' (IV. iv. 120).

Sympathy for Falstaff is further eroded by the exchange that takes place between him and the Lord Chief Justice, for although Falstaff transmutes everything that is said to him into a joke, it is plain that he does not have the upper hand. The Lord Chief Justice is not satirised here, he is presented as an honest man and an upholder of the law. Falstaff, in contrast, appears like a schoolboy caught out in a prank, and despite his ability to joke, he is not in a position of any power:

L. CHIEF JUSTICE: But since all is well, keep it so. Wake not a sleeping wolf.

FALSTAFF: To wake a wolf is as bad as smell a fox.

L. CHIEF JUSTICE: What! You are as a candle, the better part burnt out.

FALSTAFF: A wassail candle, my lord, all tallow – if I did say of wax, my growth would approve the truth.

L. CHIEF JUSTICE: There is not a white hair in your face but should have his effect of gravity.

FALSTAFF: His effect of gravy, gravy, gravy.

L. CHIEF JUSTICE: You follow the young Prince up and down, like his ill angel.

(I. ii. 155–66)

Five scenes pass before the young prince finally makes his appearance – three involving Falstaff and two involving the rebels – by which time the sense of corruption and misery is firmly established. Nor is Henry presented as an antidote to the ills of the kingdom. The introduction of Henry introduces another negative theme, that of true emotion and hypocrisy and the difficulty of distinguishing between them. Referring to his father's illness, Prince Henry protests that he is far removed from Falstaff and that his heart bleeds inwardly for his father, even though he cannot show it. When Poins asks why he cannot, Prince Henry turns the question back on him:

PRINCE: What wouldst thou think of me if I should weep?
POINS: I would think thee a most princely hypocrite.
PRINCE: It would be every man's thought.

(II. ii. 52–5)

The problem of Prince Henry's hypocrisy continues to be the subject of debate. If the plays are taken as a trilogy, then what we have is a character who appears either to undergo radical changes of personality or who is basically a chameleon, a man cast in the true Machiavellian mode who adjusts to circumstances as they alter around him. He is the man who jokes with Falstaff, wins his affection and then repudiates him in the famous 'I know thee not, old man' speech that has disturbed so many readers of the play, and he is the man who ruthlessly orders the killing of French prisoners out of military expediency. Yet that Machiavellianism is absent from the scenes in *Henry V* which deal with Henry as a lover. Offering himself as the plain dealing, down-to-earth Englishman to Katherine of France, Henry claims that he has no words with which to flatter, but instead offers honesty:

a good heart, Kate, is the sun and the moon – or rather, the sun, and not the moon; for it shines bright and never changes, but takes his course truly. If thou would have such a one, take me; and take me, take a soldier, take a soldier, take a king.

(V. ii. 161–6)

Stephen Greenblatt argues that in order to understand the conception of Prince Henry through his various manifestations, 'we need in effect a poetics of Elizabethan power'[5] and this proposition is certainly more viable than the approach which insists that the plays are about the development of a single character. Both *Henry IV, Part 2* and *Henry V* depict a wide cross-section of people and a wide range of situations – court and tavern, council of rulers and groups of rebels, battlefield and bedroom, raw recruits and experienced soldiers. In *Henry V* there is also the sustained comparison between the French and the English and there are the representatives of different places in the British Isles, the four captains – Fluellen, Gower, Jamy and Macmorris. This range of characters and settings reinforces the view that the focus of attention in both these plays is not confined to character and story. Rather they are both plays about the state of the nation, and the protagonist appears to be the mythical personification of England.

In his study of playgoing in Shakespeare's London, Andrew Gurr notes that through the 1590s the popular playhouses picked up on current issues and people in the news in much the same way as the popular press today runs features on items deemed newsworthy. He points out that history plays were extremely popular, with the figure of Falstaff as the favourite, and that during the years between 1594 and 1599, 'when the only food for playgoers was provided by the two adult companies playing at the north and south of the City', the range of plays offered was strikingly narrow, with Tamburlaine and various imitations on the one hand, and English history on the other.[6]

A consideration of the background to *Henry IV, Part 2* and *Henry V* shows therefore that although he may have enjoyed relative stability, Shakespeare was also working within certain constraints, not least of which was to provide plays with strong audience appeal. In creating the figure of Falstaff, Shakespeare created a character that dominated the stage and subverted aesthetic criteria; as a showman, he must have recognised that Falstaff was a theatrical winner and attempted to exploit this advantage to the maximum. Nevertheless, Falstaff has been killed off in *Henry V*, a detail that has puzzled generations of critics used to thinking of Shakespeare's writing as aesthetically coherent. What seems likely, however, is that Falstaff died for the same reasons that characters in contemporary soap operas occasionally die – because the actor who created the role moved elsewhere.

David Wiles, who has argued very convincingly that Falstaff
was Will Kemp's part, points out that Kemp defected to the rival
Worcester's company around the time of the composition of
Henry V, and, moreover, was probably responsible for pirating
the comedy in which Falstaff also features, *The Merry Wives of
Windsor*.[7] If this is the case, and Kemp was gone, leaving the
company with no one able to take over the role of Falstaff,
Shakespeare would not only have had to take the course of
action that the play suggests, and write out Falstaff, though with
maximum effect, milking the account of his deathbed for all the
sentiment he could, but he would also have had to provide
alternatives with strong audience appeal. If we look at *Henry V*,
those alternatives seem to have been provided not by means of
another character, but by the creation of a series of sequences
that have exceptionally powerful emotional appeal, principle of
which is the sense of patriotism.

In the late twentieth century, after two world wars and a series
of disastrous colonial and post-colonial wars, patriotism has
become a troublesome concept in the English-speaking world. In
1914 the idea of fighting for king and country was generally
accepted, but in 1982 when Britain went to war against Argen-
tina, attempts to revive the discourse of patriotism proved
deeply embarrassing. The use of national flags in western
Europe has come to signify a reactionary political stance, perhaps
even a fascist stance, and in an age of internationalism it is
difficult even to define patriotism in terms that are meaningful
without being divisive.

Henry V is a play in which patriotism is of crucial importance.
Henry is able to lead his men into battle because they share with
him the common heritage of their Englishness:

>   And you, good yeomen,
> Whose limbs were made in England, show us here
> The mettle of your pasture; let us swear
> That you are worth your breeding – which I doubt not;
> For there is none of you so mean and base
> That hath not noble lustre in your eyes.
> I see you stand like greyhounds in the slips,
> Straining upon the start. The game's afoot!
> Follow your spirit, and upon this charge

Cry, 'God for Harry, England, and Saint George!'
                                        (III. ii. 25–34)

Laurence Olivier's 1945 film version of the play, coming as it
did at the end of the Second World War, picked up on the discourse of patriotism that was in the air with the conclusion of the
long struggle against the Nazis. The film also established *Henry
V* as a classic popular text in a way that is quite unique. The
image of the feeble effeminate French court, contrasted with the
down-to-earth sensible English camp, appealed to chauvinistic
British audiences, while Olivier played Henry without ambiguities, as a man of the people, a king with the heart of a common
man and the courage of a superhero.

By 1989, with Kenneth Branagh's film version of *Henry V*, the
mood was different, and so the figure of the king is more
complex. Patriotism of the jingoistic kind had little place in the
divided society that was Britain at the end of a decade of
Thatcherism, so the task became how best to deal with the
unpopular theme of patriotism without resorting to clichés or
unpleasantly regressive ideology. The play that had worked well
in a Britain coming to the end of a long war could not be
expected to work in the same way in a Britain with one foot in
the pool of the European community.

The relationship of these two twentieth-century versions of
the play is important in terms of our understanding of the *Henry
V* of 1599. The play was written just before the departure of the
Earl of Essex for Ireland, to endeavour to suppress the rebellion
of Hugh O'Neill, the Earl of Tyrone. Throughout Elizabeth's
reign, Ireland had continued to be a source of anxiety, and after
the Babington plot, the execution of Mary Stuart in 1587 and the
abortive invasion by Spain in 1588, the presence of an un-
derdeveloped Catholic population so close to home became
increasingly problematic. Essex was sent to Ireland after many
delays with a huge army, the largest army mustered during
Elizabeth's entire reign, with some 16,000 footsoldiers and 1300
cavalry. The whole enterprise was unpopular in the country as a
whole, partly because of the vast expense that further burdened
a nation under great financial pressure, and partly because there
was widespread contempt for corrupt practices in the army that
were common knowledge. The Irish campaign was therefore the

subject of considerable ambiguity – on the one hand, the Irish and their religion were disliked and regarded as little more than barbarians, which meant that military intervention against them was uncontroversial, whilst on the other hand, there was discontent at the cost of the campaign. A parallel in the twentieth century can be found if we look at the involvement of the United States in Vietnam, when a large sum of money was put into the war effort that was at first supported as a patriotic act, but later increasingly condemned as unnecessary and morally wrong.

This was the background to the composition of *Henry V*, and it is likely that audiences would have seen the play with the Irish campaign foregrounded in their consciousness. And in case any doubt remained in anyone's mind, the prologue to act V refers directly to the Essex campaign, suggesting that he will return in triumph and be welcomed by the people of London as their hero:

> As, by a lower but loving likelihood,
> Were now the General of our gracious Empress –
> As in good time he may – from Ireland coming,
> Bringing rebellion broached on his sword,
> How many would the peaceful city quit
> To welcome him! Much more, and much more cause,
> Did they this Harry.
>
> (V. Chorus. 29–35)

Besides the parallels with the Irish campaign, the four captains who represent England, Scotland, Wales and Ireland are archetypal comic figures, who still exist today in jokes and anecdotes. Fluellen, the Welshman, features more prominently than the others, no doubt to reinforce the Welsh origins of Henry himself, who actually declares himself to be a Welshman rather than an Englishman. Jamy and Macmorris are depicted as hot-tempered, with Jamy the argumentative Scot and Macmorris the Irishman continually threatening to cut off heads or cut throats. As the play progresses, the Scotsman and the Irishman diminish in importance, a reflection of popular English sentiment, which could just about extend an acceptance to the Welsh, but regarded the Scots and the Irish as foreigners and savages. Yet with the

war in Ireland an ongoing concern, and with the Scottish King
James waiting in Edinburgh for his cousin Elizabeth to die so
that he could assume the thrones of both Scotland and England,
the prospect of a united body of four nations had never been so
imminent. Subsumed in the notion of 'England', the nation that
Henry champions, are Wales, Scotland and Ireland, all of which
are seen as owing their allegiance to the English king.

In their essay on history and ideology in *Henry V*, Jonathan
Dollimore and Alan Sinfield suggest that the principle preoccupation of the play is with insurrection:

> The King is faced with actual or threatened insurrection from
> almost every quarter: the Church, 'treacherous' fractions from
> within the ruling class, slanderous subjects, and soldiers who
> undermine the war effort, either by exploiting it or by
> sceptically interrogating the King's motives. All these areas of
> possible resistance in the play had their counterparts in Eliza-
> bethan England.[8]

This is certainly valid, but what makes *Henry V* different from
the other history plays, all of which deal with the question of
insurrection and of the conflict that arises if an anointed king is
perceived as not fit to govern his people, is the emphasis on
English identity. The need to establish a sense of identity derives
from the precariousness even of a monarch apparently as strong
as Henry after his French triumph. The conclusion to the play
reminds us, as it served to remind Elizabethan audiences, that
despite Henry's victory, the son that Henry hopes for with
Katherine, the boy 'half French, half English, that shall go to
Constantinople and take the Turk by the beard' (V. ii. 204–5), will
lose everything that has been gained:

> Henry the Sixth, in infant bands crowned King
> Of France and England, did this King succeed,
> Whose state so many had the managing
> That they lost France, and made his England bleed:
> Which oft our stage hath shown . . .
>
> (Epilogue 9–13)

Patriotism in *Henry V* serves a multifarious purpose: the story of the famous victory of the hero king would undoubtedly attract an audience, and if that audience was disappointed by the absence of Falstaff, then the presence of several old and new comic characters, together with stirring monologues by the hero would still ensure success. At the same time, the war in Ireland, which was a great drain on public money in an economy very far from buoyant, raised important questions about patriotism and about what it meant to be an Englishman. The century was coming to a close and Elizabeth had been on the throne over forty years, which meant that predictions for the future of the nation were the subject of frequent speculation. The obvious successor, if one discounted Essex himself (and we have no way of knowing whether Shakespeare did discount him) was a Scotsman who had never set foot in England, son of the woman executed for treason some twelve years previously. There was need for fresh analysis not only of what it meant to be king, but also of what it might mean to be English. Patriotism in *Henry V* is not a simple matter, and Dollimore and Sinfield are right to reject the simplistic reading that sees foreign wars as 'straight-forward ground on which to establish and celebrate national unity'[9] – though obviously this is exactly what Laurence Olivier did do, and in a context where audiences had experienced foreign war as a vehicle for a new sense of national unity, his version of the play was an enormous success.

Nevertheless, the play seems to be dealing with more than insurrection. *Henry IV, Part 2* opens with the rebels waiting for news of their fortunes, and to this extent it can be argued that the theme of insurrection runs through both plays. But the plays both contain various dramatic devices that move us away from linearity in the development of plot and character or from any thematic consistency. Insurrection is only one of the dangers faced by the king in *Henry V*, and we could equally sustain the view that in Fluellen, Gower, Montjoy, Burgundy and Katherine we have a range of examples of loyalty, chivalry and affection that can be set against the negative examples also contained within the play.

The Chorus who opens and closes the play reminds us of two things – of the need for imagination which transforms the immediately visible and makes it into something other than the narrow reality within it, and the inevitability of the passing of time. Ostensibly the Chorus sets the scene, telling us what has happened and summarising events so as to move the action onwards, but each one of the Chorus's speeches urges the audience to think, to use their minds to extend the parameters of the play. It has been suggested that the Chorus has an epic function, but that notion of epic needs to be interpreted in the Brechtian sense, for the Chorus in *Henry V*, like the figure of Rumour in *Henry IV, Part 2*, is very close to the devices used by Brecht in the furtherance of his process of alienation effect. Brecht saw the parallels between his own work and Shakespeare very clearly, and suggests that both playwrights were aiming for similar goals:

> With Shakespeare the audience does the constructing. Shakespeare never bends the course of human destiny in the second act to make a fifth act possible. With him everything takes its natural course. In the lack of connection between his acts we see the lack of connection in a human destiny, when it is recounted by someone with no interest in tidying it up so as to provide an idea (which can only be a prejudice) with an argument not taken from life. There's nothing more stupid than to perform Shakespeare so that he's clear. He's by his very nature unclear. He's pure material.[10]

Both *Henry IV, Part 2* and *Henry V* are, in Brecht's terms, unclear plays. There are so many characters, so many threads of plot that are taken up and then dropped again, so many changes of scene, so many shifts of focus that our attention is continually diverted in a kaleidoscopic manner. This must surely be deliberate; by the end of the 1590s Shakespeare was a very experienced man of the theatre, not averse to formal experiments or risk-taking, so we can assume that he knew exactly what he was doing. The lack of clarity is part of the structure of these two plays, which offer us a panoramic view of a society rather than an in-depth study of characters. The society depicted in both plays is similar, though with significant differences. In *Henry IV, Part 1*, the emphasis is on the need for sound moral principles combined with resoluteness as a remedy for society's ills. Once elevated to king, Henry takes justice, personified by the Lord Chief Justice, as his symbolic father:

> Now call we our high court of parliament,
> And let us choose such limbs of noble counsel
> That the great body of our state may go
> In equal rank, with the best-governed nation;
> That war, or peace, or both at once, may be
> As things acquainted and familiar to us;
> In which you, father, shall have foremost hand.
>   (V. ii. 134–40)

This newly adopted father seals Falstaff's doom, for Falstaff from the outset of the play has been presented as the antithesis of the Lord Chief Justice. Mistress Quickly, Doll Tearsheet, Falstaff and all his friends are arrested in a symbolic cleansing process, though the apparent severity of this measure is offset by Prince John's remark that Henry intends all his former friends to be well provided for and that they are to be banished until they have undergone a form of re-education, 'till their conversations/Appear more wise and modest to the world'.

If *Henry IV, Part 2* emphasises the need for a moral basis of good government, *Henry V* suggests that other requirements are also essential – loyalty, a sense of patriotism, unity and, above all, obedience. The much discussed moment in IV. vi, where Henry orders the immediate execution of the French prisoners is an example of these virtues in action. Henry's order, which, as Fluellen points out, is expressly against the law of arms, has been taken by some critics as further evidence of Henry's coldness and hypocrisy. The scene between Fluellen and Gower that follows the order is highly comic, and this juxtaposition of comedy and barbarity can be difficult for twentieth-century sensibilities to accept. However, Holinshed's source text explains the necessity of this brutal action and Shakespeare's play offers it without explanation as an example of the need for soldiers to show absolute obedience to their general on the field of battle. Immediately after the order to execute the prisoners, Henry is shown at his best, when he humbly acknowledges the hand of God in granting him victory and accedes to the French herald's request for the defeated army to bury their dead with honour.

Henry IV, Part 2 poses the question of what a king should be and how a nation should be ruled in time of peace (relative peace, that is, for the threat of rebellion is always present) while *Henry V* looks at how a nation should be governed in time of war. It is significant that in both these pictures of society, the role of women is marginal. In *Henry IV, Part 2* both Lady Percy and Doll Tearsheet in their different ways preach restraint, with Lady Percy persuading her father-in-law to flee to Scotland and abandon his rebellion and Doll reminding Falstaff that he is old and coming closer to death every day.

In *Henry V* the role of women is even more stylised. The French, who are presented throughout the play as the enemy, speak in English in the interests of dramatic consistency. But Katherine speaks only in French until her few faltering attempts at English in act V, and so she becomes the physical embodiment of otherness: she is French and she is woman, the enemy and the unknown, and like all women she has no place at all in the theatre of war. Mistress Quickly, the other female character of any substance in the play, represents another aspect of the feminine – compassion. Her account of Falstaff's death in II. iii is very moving, but after this scene she disappears, and towards the end of the play we hear that she died of the pox. War is a man's business and women have no central role to play. Compassion, like love-making, are permissible in times of peace, but when the blast of war blows, as Henry tells us, fair nature must be disguised with hard-favoured rage.

Henry IV, Part 2 and *Henry V* are not likeable plays; they disturb too much, and unlike the later tragedies, which also disturb, there is no emotional investment in a protagonist like a Hamlet, an Othello, a Macbeth or a Lear. The diffuseness of both plays and their complex structuring also signals the difference between these two works and other plays by Shakespeare. Yet it is interesting to note that both have provided the basis for highly successful films – Olivier's *Henry V* and, more recently, Branagh's version, and Orson Welles's compilation of the two parts of *Henry IV* in his *Chimes at Midnight* (1966). Despite their rootedness in Elizabethan society, these plays are very open-ended and this serves to make them accessible to other cultures in other times. For in his analysis of a society in a state of uneasiness, caught between colonial wars and economic decline, Shakespeare described a phenomenon that is all too familiar even in our own supposedly enlightened, technological times.

7
The Play's the Thing:
The Merry Wives of Windsor

When Stephen Greenblatt suggested that what was needed to understand Shakespeare's conception of Prince Henry was a poetics of Elizabethan power, he also added that this would prove 'inseparable, in crucial respects, from a poetics of the theatre'.[1] For the figure of the ruler in Elizabethan England was essentially theatrical, and Elizabeth herself was shrewdly aware of her presence on the stage of England as a principle performer. Before she came to the throne in 1558, during the years of her sister Mary's rule, she had skilfully demonstrated her performance abilities even in times of the greatest danger. Released from the Tower of London and banished to Woodstock in Oxfordshire in 1554, Elizabeth's journey into exile was a triumph of theatricality. People threw flowers at her and rang bells and at Wycombe she is said to have been given so many cakes and breads that she had to ask people to stop because there was too much to carry. Her coronation four years later was an extraordinary display of pageantry, and throughout her reign her progresses around the country served to remind the people that she was still visibly in power. Yet, despite this process of displaying herself as the living sign of queen to the people, at the same time she and her government were engaged in setting up invisible structures of power. Walsingham's secret police and international spying network was organised on an unprecedented scale, and it is in this duality, this contrast between the trappings of power and the concealed mechanics of power that we can see evidence of what Foucault has analysed as the great disjunction that marks the end of the Renaissance.[2]

The image of the world as a stage, of the ruler as actor pervades Shakespeare's plays. Generations of readers, critics, members of audiences have responded to that imagery, but it is only when the plays are transformed into performances that the other side of the metaphor appears. For just as the state was run on a combination of visible and invisible structures of power, so the theatre functions in the same way. An audience encounters the visible product, the play in performance, but the actors know what that process of making visible involves. The mechanics of staging, the actors' training, the financial constraints, the limitations imposed by censorship all contributed (as they still do today) in unseen ways to shaping the play that eventually appeared in the theatre.

When a playwright chooses to expose those invisible processes and bring them to the attention of the audience, thereby destroying the illusion of reality on which mimetic theatre rests, the result is self-conscious theatre that may also be self-examining. It is striking to note how frequently Shakespeare chose to do just that, with the result that a great many of his plays are effectively metatexts, or plays about theatre.

Henry V opens with the Chorus apologising for the inadequacy of the theatre as a place to display the great drama that is about to unfold:

> But pardon, gentles all,
> The flat unraised spirits that hath dared
> On this unworthy scaffold to bring forth
> So great an object. Can this cockpit hold
> The vasty fields of France? Or may we cram
> Within this wooden O the very casques
> That did affright the air at Agincourt?
> (Prologue. 8–14)

The only way to deal with this unresolvable problem, says the

Chorus, is for the audience to let their 'imaginary forces work', and he reappears at the start of each subsequent act to remind them to continue to use their imaginations, stretching beyond the boundaries of the stage.

In 1581, the Master of Revels was granted wide powers of censorship. All licensed players were to obtain his approval, submitting

> all such plays, tragedies, comedies, or shows, as they shall have in readiness, or mean to set forth, and them to present and recite before our said servant, or his sufficient deputy, whom we ordain, appoint, and authorise by these presents, of all such shows, plays, players, and playmakers, together with their playing places, to order and reform, authorise and put down, as shall be thought meet or unmeet unto himself, or his said deputy in that behalf.[3]

In 1598, a privy council edict restricted the London companies to two, in a move that did away with a number of minor theatres and the City Inns. This state of affairs did not last long, and two new adult companies were quickly formed, followed by the return of two companies of boy players, but on different terms, for now besides the public playing spaces there also arose private ones. Andrew Gurr discusses the difference between the public spaces used by the adult companies and the private spaces used by the boys, pointing out that the adults used to perform either in public amphitheatres ('as rivals to the bulls and bears') or in private halls if commissioned to do so.[4] The adult companies had very simple staging requirements and could set up and perform more or less anywhere:

> Quite contrary to this were the 'private' houses, where the boy companies acted, and which the adults did not acquire until 1609. Being set in the halls of existing buildings their capacities were far smaller than those of the wooden amphitheatres, perhaps no more than five or six hundred. Their performances were candle-lit, their prices for admission were at least six times as high, and above all they reversed the priorities in the auditorium. There was no standing, and the cheapest seats were those in the galleries, 'the gods'. In

comfort, and in seating layout they were fitted out for the wealthy. The Restoration theatres copied their auditorium arrangement, in preference to that of the public amphi-theatres, and started a tradition of theatre design which has lasted down to today.[5]

In the last years of the sixteenth century and the first decade of the seventeenth, great changes were taking place in the London theatres, in terms of company structures, playing spaces, control of the censors and, as a result of all that, designated audiences. At the same time, great changes were taking place in the relationship between visible manifestations of power and the invisible networks that were being devised in order to ensure the security of government. Great changes also took place in Shakespeare's life, and for once there is evidence that is based on more than surmise: in 1599 the lease for the new Globe Theatre was signed and Shakespeare's name appeared as one of the collective of owners, entitled to 10 per cent of the rights.

Muriel Bradbrook has suggested that Shakespeare developed his 'new imaginative delicate comedy' as a response to the rise of the boy companies with their 'snarling satire'. To support her argument, she lists the following titles of plays for the years 1597–1601: *Henry V, The Merry Wives of Windsor, Much Ado About Nothing, As You Like It, Twelfth Night, Julius Caesar* and *Hamlet*.[6] But while she quite rightly notes the move from history plays to other forms, what seems more noteworthy about the plays that she lists is their consistent preoccupation with theatre itself rather than any common thematic link. In *Henry V*, the Chorus is a constant reminder of the artificiality of the theatrical moment, the plots of the comedies are structured around disguising and dissembling, *Julius Caesar* examines the paradox of the truth of rhetoric and the rhetoric of truth, while in *Hamlet* a troupe of professional actors are introduced onto the stage as part of the action of the play. Whether consciously or uncon-sciously, the plays between 1597 and 1601 are all plays about playing roles.

The moral function that theatre can have is demonstrated in *Hamlet*; the Players are asked by Hamlet to stage a reenactment of the murder of his father by Claudius in an attempt to stir Claudius's guilty conscience. Hamlet's instructions to the Players provide an opportunity for a statement about contemporary acting, and about some of the excesses to be seen and heard on the Elizabethan stage. Hamlet warns the Players against bad diction and useless gesture, about exaggerated stylisation and excessive improvisation. (In view of the defection of Kemp from Shakespeare's company around this time, one wonders if there might not be a deliberate, rather spiteful joke here when Hamlet accuses clowns who try too hard for audience response which 'shows a most pitiful ambition in the fool that uses it'.) In these instructions Hamlet also defines the purpose of performing:

> the purpose of playing, whose end, both at the first and now, was and is to hold as 'twere the mirror up to nature, to show virtue her own feature, scorn her own image, and the very age and body of the time his form and pressure. Now this overdone, or come tardy off, though it make the unskilful laugh, cannot but make the judicious grieve; the censure of the which one must in your allowance o'erweigh a whole theatre of others. (III. ii. 20–8)

Those critics who have argued that Shakespeare's theatre was apolitical have obviously failed to comprehend what theatre signified to the Elizabethan audience. Far from being depoliticised, theatre was as politically charged as the ballad or broadsheet, and the stage offered an opportunity for the public discussion of contentious issues (within the boundaries proscribed by the censors, of course).

The use of the metaphor of the world as a stage and human beings as players raised questions about appearance and reality, about the relationship between truth and disguise. In *A Midsummer Night's Dream*, Snug the joiner feels that he must dispel any illusion that he might indeed be a real lion when he comes on to begin his part:

> You, ladies, you whose gentle hearts do fear
> The smallest monstrous mouse that creeps on floor,
> May now perchance both quake and tremble here
> When lion rough in wildest rage doth roar.
> Then know that I as Snug the joiner am
> A lion fell, nor else no lion's dam.

For if I should as Lion come in strife
Into this place, 'twere pity on my life.

                    (V. i. 217–24)

To which Theseus remarks that the speaker is 'a very gentle beast, and of good conscience'.

The breaking of illusion in the last act of *A Midsummer Night's Dream* is comic parody, in contrast to the similar rupture that occurs through *Henry V*. But the function of both these self-conscious statements about the illusory nature of theatre is similar, in that both plays draw attention to the presence of a hidden reality: behind the appearance of the actor is a real person, behind the illusion of the play is a complex network of economic, technical and managerial skills that make its appearance on a stage possible, behind the pageant of the state occasion is the machinery that enables those in power to remain where they want to be.

The plays written between 1597 and 1601 are more self-consciously metatheatrical than most of Shakespeare's output, though obviously the metaphor of the world as a stage runs through a great many other plays throughout his career, and works as diverse as *The Taming of the Shrew* and *The Tempest* display processes of staging at work in the course of the play. Indeed, one way to deal with the problem of Shakespeare's apparent misogyny in *The Taming of the Shrew* is to interpret the play as a dream sequence, a device that critics justify by giving prominence to the Christopher Sly scenes that serve as a frame at the start of the play.

Of the plays from this period, however, the one that is least discussed in terms of its metatheatricality is *The Merry Wives of Windsor*, perhaps because it fits less comfortably into any category and is somewhat outside the pattern of the other six plays. It is a comedy, but not a romantic comedy, and might more fairly be described as a citizens' comedy. It is set in a recognisable English milieu, with a cast of stock comic characters – the jealous husband, the clownish suitor, the witty, quick-thinking older woman, the romantic hero and heroine, the incompetent justice, the Welsh parson, the French doctor and, of course, Falstaff and Bardolph, Nym and Pistol, his followers.

There is a story that suggests that *The Merry Wives of Windsor* was written expressly at the Elizabeth's command, because 'She was so well pleas'd with that admirable Character of Falstaff, in the two Parts of Henry the Fourth, that she commanded him to continue it for one Play more, and to shew him in Love.'[7] This story is first recorded in 1702, so its authenticity is questionable, but along with the suggestion that the play was expressly commissioned by the queen is another story, which relates how Shakespeare wrote the play for performance within a fortnight. The 1602 Quarto does say that the play had been performed before her majesty 'divers times', but the information about the queen wanting to see Falstaff in love and about the fortnight's composition time only appeared a century after the play's first appearance. The story is consistent with later interpretations of the play, which place Falstaff in the central role, so that the action becomes an extended romp, with Falstaff as the buffoon and the other characters located in relation to him. But if we read the play this way, then there are inconsistencies that are somewhat perplexing, for although Falstaff is a strong comic figure the focus of the play is by no means all directed towards him.

H. J. Oliver points out that *The Merry Wives of Windsor* 'may be seen as a superb medley of all that would be likely to amuse an aristocratic audience towards the close of the sixteenth century'.[8] This assessment of the play directs our attention to Shakespeare's craftmanship, his skill as a writer of hit shows, in other words, his ability to appeal to the market-place. *The Merry Wives of Windsor* employs a whole range of theatrical strategies designed to ensure its success, and if the play were written in a short time, as seems likely, then it is all the more revealing as an example of Shakespeare's technical ability.

Literary critics and those who insist on seeing Shakespeare primarily as the creator of 'Great Art' tend to shy away from a consideration of Shakespeare as commercial script-writer, though this is precisely what he was. Although *The Merry Wives of Windsor* may not have been written expressly at the queen's command, it was probably written for the occasion of a feast to celebrate the installation of the Lord Chamberlain as Knight of the Garter in 1597, an event that took place at Windsor. Moreover, speed in writing and putting on plays was an essential prerequisite for the commercial companies. An examination of the Admiral's Company, for example, shows that in the season of 1594–5 they performed six days a week with a repertoire of thirty-eight plays, of which twenty-one were new plays added at fortnightly intervals. The following season they performed thirty-seven plays, of which nineteen were new and in 1596–7 they performed thirty-four plays, of which fourteen were new.[9] This kind of repertory system demanded a high degree of pre-performance skill, and actors tended to have at their command a set of stock roles which they could work from, in much the same way as the *commedia* companies worked on the Continent. In the late nineteenth century, when there were still a number of travelling companies on the road in Italy, actors worked in probably much the same way as actors must have worked in Elizabethan England. Eleonora Duse, born into a family of travelling players, was put on stage as a child player at the age of four, and then moved to the position in the company of second female at a very early age. The death of her mother when Duse was only fourteen propelled her into the leading lady parts. The standard way through such a company structure was to move through juvenile roles into young hero and young heroine roles, then to the prima donna and primo attore (leading lady and leading man) and perhaps ultimately to the roles of character actor and mother. Of course not all actors made those same transitions; some stayed in secondary positions in the company and never played leading roles, whilst others played clown roles throughout their careers.

We can assume, not too unfairly, that the devising of *The Merry Wives of Windsor* utilised the skills of the company to the maximum and offered the audience a wide range of stock comic types. The comic Welshman and the comic Frenchman are caricature figures, as is the idiotic youth Slender, who woos Anne Page in such a ludicrous fashion. Falstaff is depicted as a would-be seducer with his eye on Mistress Ford, and his endeavours end in scenes of comic failure: first he is carried out ignominiously in a laundry basket, and then he is subjected to humiliating teasing by pretend fairies in the Great Park at Windsor.

It has often been noted that the Falstaff of this play bears little resemblance to the character in the Henry plays and various reasons have been advanced for this. For some time it was thought that the play dated from 1600, and so was written as a sequel to the other Falstaff plays, with the fat knight making his

comeback for his fans after Shakespeare had killed him off in
Henry V, but that view has largely been discredited. The story of
the queen asking for further adventures of Falstaff must be
discounted as legend. It seems more likely that the play was
written for the Garter celebrations, and that Shakespeare probably interrupted the writing of *Henry IV Part 2* in order to
compose it. If this is the case, then more important than Falstaff
as lover is Falstaff as inadequate knight, a comic reversal of the
values of chivalry that the Knights of the Garter were supposed
to uphold. David Wiles takes this view, but goes further and
proposes that: 'It must have appeared far more obvious, in April,
1597, that the "Falstaff" of Merry Wives was intended as a
reworking of the original Sir John Falstaff from Part One of
Henry the Sixth.'[10]

The original Sir John was stripped of his Garter medal and so
appears as the symbol of unknightly behaviour, as a knight of
Misrule, whose values are the opposite of the ideals celebrated
in the Garter ceremony. From the start, Falstaff is a symbol of
corruption and dishonesty:

> Indeed, I am in the waist two yards about; but I am now about
> no waste; I am about thrift. Briefly, I do mean to make love to
> Ford's wife: I spy entertainment in her; she discourses, she
> carves, she gives the leer of invitation: I can construe the
> action of her familiar style; and the hardest voice of her
> behaviour, to be Englished rightly, is, 'I am Sir John Falstaff's'.
> (I. ii. 42–9)

The theory that links Falstaff to the corrupt knight from an
earlier play takes us into the complexities of topical references
that have puzzled and intrigued readers for centuries. Briefly,
Shakespeare appears to have originally given his Falstaff character the name of Sir John Oldcastle, the historical character who
was companion to the young King Henry V but who was
eventually burned as a Lollard heretic. When this character first
appeared in *Henry IV, Part 1*, the descendants of the original Sir
John protested, and by the time the play was printed, the name
had been changed from Oldcastle to Falstaff. That Shakespeare
was irritated by this appears to be borne out by the epilogue to
Henry IV, Part 2, where Falstaff's death in *Henry V* is predicted,

followed by the ironic comment that 'Oldcastle died a martyr, and this is not the man'. William Brooke, Lord Cobham, whose family made the protest was at one time Lord Chamberlain, so in a position of sufficient power to ensure that the name was duly changed to avoid insult to his ancestor, but there is a possibility that Shakespeare continued to needle the Cobhams by calling Ford, the archetypal jealous husband, by the pseudonym 'Brooke', a name that in turn had to be changed and so appears as Broome in the Folio. Whatever the intricacies of these games of naming, what can be deduced is that *The Merry Wives of Windsor* would have contained a whole set of topical allusions that an audience of the day could have followed, and that the story of both Sir John Oldcastle, the heretic knight associated with *Henry IV, Part 2*, and Sir John Falstaff, the dishonourable knight, associated with Shakespeare's earlier success, *Henry VI, Part 1*, would have been present in their minds.

David Wiles suggests that Shakespeare's thinking about the names was as follows:

> I will bow to pressure. Kemp will now play a fat knight who is definitely not 'Oldcastle', but the Brooke family name will not escape untarnished because the central comic figure will be Ford alias Brooke.

and he adds that although notionally separate, the figure of Falstaff subsumes 'Oldcastle' in *Henry IV, Part 2* and so a single composite emerges:

> Many of the characters in *Merry Wives* can be seen as a first draft for their successors in *Part 2*. . . . The circumstances of the original performance explain why Falstaff in *Merry Wives* is different from Kemp's other clowns . . . his speech tends to be in elaborated code. The clown cannot establish communality with an elite audience on an official occasion. Rather, the audience are encouraged throughout to sense their superiority over the false knight. There can be no jig and, accordingly, the narrative of the clown's wooing is completed. His metamorphosis – into a stag – is enacted on stage, and he is fully integrated in the play's finale.[11]

I have quoted Wiles at some length here because his analysis
does seem to make a lot of sense, and because he approaches the
problem from the point of view of the play as theatre, rather than
as a literary text with 'inconsistencies' of plot and characterisation. The idea that Shakespeare was responding to expediency
is in accordance with the notion of Shakespeare as master crafts-
man, able to devise an entertainment for a select audience at very
short notice, structured both to utilise the company he had at his
disposal and to highlight the symbolic significance of the
occasion of its performance, besides also serving as a foretaste of
the further adventures of Falstaff, Bardolph, Pistol and Nym in
Henry I, Part 2 and *Henry V*. The comic foreigners who cannot
speak English properly, Sir Hugh Evans and Doctor Caius
reappear later also, via Fluellen and the jokes with Katherine and
her Nurse in *Henry V*. Rather than a sequel to the Henry plays,
The Merry Wives of Windsor seems to be an intermediate stage in
the development of a series of comic characters and situations.

Besides the topical allusions (the opening scene is full of them,
setting the tone of what is to follow) and the appearance of
characters who also feature in other of Shakespeare's plays, there
are references to previous stage successes by Shakespeare.
Indeed, it is possible to see *The Merry Wives of Windsor* as one of,
if not the most self-referential of all the plays, filled as it is with
theatrical clues. And although Ford is the character at the centre
of the narrative, it is Falstaff who is at the centre of the web of
metatheatrical references, as for example, when he refers to the
Elizabethan tradition of playing with boys taking women's parts.
Speaking to a boy in the role of Mistress Ford, Falstaff says:

> Come, I cannot cog and say thou art this and that, like a many
> of these lisping hawthorn-buds, that come like women in
> men's apparel and smell like Bucklersbury in simple-time.
>
> (III. iii. 63–7)

The joke is an obvious one, and works on several levels. Falstaff
is trying to present himself as an honest, plain-talking man,
when in fact he lusts after Mistress Ford; she in turn, along with
the audience, knows that Falstaff is a liar and is about to be
taught a lesson; the audience knows perfectly well that the actor
playing Mistress Ford is a male disguised as a female, and so a

parallel is made between the art of disguising that is theatre, and the deceit of disguising that happens in life. A variant of the same joke occurs in act V, when Slender and Caius both steal the 'woman' they think is Ann Page and end up with a 'great lubberly boy' in disguise instead.

The conclusion of the play pulls all the threads together. Falstaff is disguised as Herne the Hunter, wearing a buck's head with antlers (a visible sign of a cuckold, though in this case he is not actually cuckolded because he has no wife of his own) in hopes of consummating his desire for Ford's wife in the park. What he does not know is that a complicated plot has been hatched, which involves the merry wives, their followers and children disguising themselves as fairies, with a character called Mistress Quickly (though of no resemblance to the Mistress Quickly of the Henry plays) making an appearance as the Fairy Queen. The fairies all gather round Falstaff and pinch him as he cowers in terror, and in her address to her 'court', the Fairy Queen manages to combine the punishment of Falstaff with praise for a true Knight of the Garter:

> And Honi soit qui mal y pense write
> In em'rald tufts, flowers purple, blue and white,
> Like sapphire, pearl, and rich embroidery
> Buckled below fair knighthood's bending knee.
>
> (V. v. 170–3)

The fairies recall *A Midsummer Night's Dream*, and a further reminder is provided by Falstaff's remark 'I do begin to perceive that I am made an ass', which is a reference to the fate of Bottom, as well as being an accurate statement about what has happened to him.

There is another reminder of *A Midsummer Night's Dream* in the sequence that follows the exposure of Falstaff, when Page's plot to marry off his daughter to Slender, and Ann Page's plot to marry her off to Doctor Caius both come to grief. Duke Theseus came across the lovers in the first light of dawn, their differences magically resolved by a night in the enchanted Athenian forest; in the 'real' world of Windsor, the fairies are citizens in disguise and the plotting of parents comes to grief, when the 'bride' is exposed as a sham. 'By gar, I am cozened', says Doctor Caius,

who has gone a step further than Slender and actually married
his boy. In the real world, the playing of women by men is
exposed as false and ludicrous.

When Ann Page and her newly married husband Fenton
appear in the final moments of the play, Fenton's speech takes
up the theme that provides the basis for both *A Midsummer
Night's Dream* and *Romeo and Juliet* – that of forced marriage. He
addresses the parents who have tried by stealth to marry off their
daughter against her will and in secret from one another:

> You would have married her most shamefully,
> Where there was no proportion held in love.
> The truth is, she and I, long since contracted,
> Are now so sure that nothing can dissolve us.
> Th'offence is holy that she hath committed,
> And this deceit loses the name of craft,
> Of disobedience, or unduteous title
> Since therein she doth evitate and shun
> A thousand irreligious cursed hours
> Which forced marriage would have brought upon her.
>
> (V. v. 234–43)

Fenton's speech is a statement on behalf of honesty. He and Ann
have been true to their vow to one another, and have resisted the
endeavours of her parents to separate them. The parents accept
the force of circumstances and give their blessing, and the
conclusion is a happy one. Falstaff is allowed to join in the
celebrations that are promised later, and so is pardoned after
being duly punished. The play ends on a rather sedate note,
without a dance or an epilogue, but with the sound values
personified by Ann Page and Fenton strongly proclaimed. Two
young people from two different social backgrounds have been
united in love.

Critics have frequently wrestled with the problem of ascer-
taining Shakespeare's sources for *The Merry Wives of Windsor*.
There are no clear sources and it seems more likely that Shakespeare drew for inspiration on his own native wit rather than
adapting an extant play or other literary text. The topicality of
the play and the references to other Shakespearean plays of the
period suggest that he was using his own work as the source

material, adapting situations and characters, shaping a comic celebration that would suit the particular occasion for which it was commissioned.

If Falstaff is presented in this play as an example of un-knightliness, so as to throw into better light the qualities of the new Knight of the Garter, so also is the metaphor of the world as a stage presented from an alternative perspective. Falstaff, the merry wives, Ford and the suitors are all playing roles and all stand, in the end, confounded before the honest openness of the young lovers who are located solidly in the real world of English citizenship. When the lovers discuss Page's objections to Fenton's suit because he is a young man from the upper classes fallen upon hard times and trying to win himself a wealthy bourgeois wife, Fenton tells Ann 'thou must be thyself', and then admits that he did at first court her for her money but has since

> found thee of more value
> Than stamps in gold or sums in sealed pages;
> And 'tis the very riches of thyself
> That now I aim at.
>
> (III. iv. 15–18)

Fenton, the former dissolute young aristocrat, becomes the spokesman for honest dealings, in love and in the world, standing up against parental double-dealing and stating the case for freedom of choice as opposed to enforced contract. It is tempting to see in this a suggestion that the landed aristocracy embodies virtues that the new emergent bourgeoisie would do well to follow. When the Host describes Fenton in terms that depict him as an ideal lover, Page gives materialistic reasons for his opposition:

HOST: What say you to young Master Fenton? He capers, he dances, he has eyes of youth; he writes verses, he speaks holiday, he smells April and May. He will carry't, he will carry't; 'tis in his buttons he will carry't.

PAGE: Not by my consent, I promise you. The gentleman is of no having: he kept company with the wild Prince and Poins. He is of too high a region; he knows too much. No, he shall not knit a knot in his fortunes with the finger of

> my substance; if he takes her, let him take her simply: the
> wealth I have waits on my consent, and my consent goes
> not that way.
>
> (III. ii. 63–75)

There is another reference here to one of Shakespeare's plays, the
popular *Henry IV, Part 1*, used to signal two contrasting views.
On the one hand, the debauchery of the young prince and his
companions is a central issue in the play, but by the end it is clear
that Henry is by no means what he seems and his lifestyle in
the taverns is exposed as a form of disguise. Page, however, is
only able to read surface signs, and so is several stages behind
the audience who know that Henry (and by association Fenton)
is indeed worthy. The audience is therefore invited to laugh
at Page, with his bourgeois limitations and restricted understanding, and as a result Fenton is cast in an even more favourable light. Fenton's declaration of love for Ann, which is also
a renunciation of his past wildness is comparable to Henry's
renunciation of his past as he moves towards becoming a worthy
king.

The Merry Wives of Windsor is an unusual play in that it stands
somewhat outside the other Shakespearean plays of the period,
and yet is related to them in all sorts of ways: by the appearance
of characters who also appear elsewhere, by theme, by
cross-referencing, by self-conscious reminders of the fact that the
play is written by Shakespeare, the playwright responsible for a
number of other successes. It is arguably the one Shakespeare
play that is most definitely located in a recognizable Elizabethan
society, and consequently it presents problems for later audiences and readers. Interestingly, it has provided the basis of a
number of operas, which perhaps shows that the narrative
structure is very strong, despite the difficulties of the language.

Leaving a recent production of *The Merry Wives of Windsor* in
the main theatre at Stratford-upon-Avon, a group of people who
had been in the audience were loudly proclaiming the timel-
essness of Shakespeare. The comedy of the play had come across
magnificently, they were saying, the theatre had been filled
with laughter, the play had survived the test of centuries.
Shakespeare's humour was our humour, there were no barriers
to understanding. But what they had not perceived about the

production was that the performers had resorted to all kinds of physical devices in order to help the audience with a text that was often obscure, at times completely meaningless. By inserting comic stage business here and there, the actors tried to compensate for Shakespeare's text, thereby showing not that it had survived the test of time but rather than it was so firmly anchored in Elizabethan England that twentieth-century England could only hazily reach out to touch it. Acting techniques learned centuries after the death of Shakespeare and his players provided a form of 'translation' for the play, and the laughter that shook the auditorium owed more to those techniques than to the obscure verbal humour of a play composed for an élite group gathered together on an élite occasion and familiar with all the coded references, in-jokes and topicalities that are encoded into the action.

The Merry Wives of Windsor is a play of its time, a play that we can reach principally through forms of translation, which does not mean that it is an archaic curiosity, or that it has deserved the marginal treatment it has so often received by critics who cannot comfortably locate it in relation to the other romantic comedies of the period. Rather, it should be seen as an example of Shakespeare's stagecraft, of his skill in devising a play at short notice for a specific public and making that play work on all sorts of levels. It is another indication of the high point that Shakespeare had reached by the late 1590s as an Elizabethan showman.

8
Love and Disillusionment:
As You Like It and
Twelfth Night

As You Like It and *Twelfth Night* are widely considered the high points of Shakespeare's comedy, yet both have suffered from an overly sentimental approach which persists in seeing the plays as glorious love stories in idyllic settings. 'There is something almost akin to fairyland . . . in the half-heavenly Forest of Arden' was Swinburne's verdict of *As You Like It* in 1909, and as late as 1962, Dover Wilson listed both plays as among Shakespeare's 'happy' comedies.[1] The roles of Rosalind and Viola in particular have offered generations of leading ladies an opportunity to show off their talents in a breeches part and the plays are high on the list of those performed regularly by schools, by amateur groups and in provincial repertory, most of which tend to emphasise the light-heartedness of the plays. A great many productions of *Twelfth Night*, for example, have managed to avoid the ambiguities of the opening scene, where the melancholy Orsino calls for music, by following Kemble's example of 1810, and opening the play with the shipwreck, thereby making Viola into the principal character who enters with the famous question 'What country, friends, is this?' and who then becomes the central focus of attention in the action that follows.

Both plays take us through a tangled maze of complication in love stories, and end with lovers happily united. Rosalind and Orlando, Celia and Oliver, the aristocratic lovers all come together, as do Silvius and Phoebe, the pastoral couple and Touchstone and Audrey, the clown pair who are 'as sure together/As the winter to foul weather' and all join the dance that concludes *As You Like It*. In *Twelfth Night*, Viola wins her love, Orsino, while Sebastian and Olivia are united. If comedy requires a conclusion that ties up ends and restores order, then certainly so far as the love stories go, both plays have splendidly comic conclusions.

Jan Kott, however, saw another, much darker side to these two plays, one that a number of earlier critics, who had seen much more than romantic stories leading to joyous conclusions, had also perceived in various ways. In both plays, the action takes place against a background of darkness and injustice. In both there are prominent figures whose unhappiness and sense of disillusionment with the world disturbs the joy – characters such as Malvolio and Feste the Clown in *Twelfth Night*, or Jaques in *As You Like It*. Malvolio's last words, after he has been exposed and punished by the conspiracy of Sir Toby Belch, Sir Andrew Aguecheek, Maria and Feste are: 'I'll be revenged on the whole pack of you' (V. i. 380), while Jaques goes off to join the Duke who has 'put on a religious life/And thrown into neglect the pompous court' (V. iv. 181–2).

Kott suggests that *As You Like It* appears to forecast *King Lear*:

Sometimes one has the impression that Shakespeare has in fact written three or four plays and kept repeating the same themes in different registers and keys, until he broke with all harmony in the *musique concrète* of *King Lear*. The storm came upon Lear and made him go mad in the same forest of Arden where, not so long ago, in *As You Like It*, another exiled prince, another exiled brother, and a pair of lovers, had deluded themselves that they would find freedom, security and happiness. Exiled princes are accompanied by clowns; or rather, by one and the same clown. Touchstone knows very well that the Forest of Arden is only an illusion, that there is no escape from the world's cruelty.[2]

This interpretation sees the play as concerned with much more than sexual fulfilment, and when Kott compares *Twelfth Night* to Genet's *The Maids* he similarly reminds us that the play is by no means all gaiety. There are too many signals in both plays that disrupt the pastoral idyll; in *Twelfth Night* there is the shipwreck and Viola's fear that her brother is drowned, Olivia is in mourning for her own dead brother, plague lurks in the background from the opening scene, when Orsino praises Olivia with the ambiguous lines:

> O, when mine eyes did see Olivia first,
> Methought she purg'd the air of pestilence;
> That instant was I turn'd into a hart,
> And my desires, like fell and cruel hounds,
> E'er since pursue me.
>
> (I. i. 19–23)

The gulling of Malvolio turns into persecution, as the man we have delighted to see humiliated because of his overbearing behaviour and snobbishness becomes a victim of his victims' revenge. The Clown leads the persecution of Malvolio, and it is obvious that the Clown in this play is a 'bitter fool'. His song, presented by way of an Epilogue, takes up the motif of inclement weather; besides the plague and the tempests that cast ships up on the shore of Illyria, 'the rain it raineth every day'.

As You Like It has even darker undertones, despite the ending that brings four pairs of lovers together. The play opens with an angry meeting between Orlando and his elder brother Oliver. Orlando accuses Oliver of betraying the trust their father placed in him and claims that he is being deprived of the education and status he deserves – 'call you that keeping, for a gentleman of my birth, that differs not from the stalling of an ox?' (I. i. 13). Oliver and Orlando quarrel violently, and Oliver also turns on the old servant, Adam, who is a father-figure, calling him an 'old dog'. The parallels with the biblical sons of Adam, Cain and Abel are thus firmly established, and it comes as no surprise later in the same scene when we find Oliver trying to arrange for Charles, the wrestler, to break Orlando's neck in the forthcoming wrestling bout. Charles also brings news of a second Cain and Abel story: the old duke, father to Rosalind, has been banished by his younger brother, the new duke, and Rosalind has only been allowed to remain because of her close friendship to her cousin, Celia. The old duke is said to have gone into the Forest of Arden, 'and there they live like the old Robin Hood of England' (I. i. 117).

The idyllic life of the Forest of Arden, however, soon proves to be as illusory as the ideal of harmony in families. As the duke says, 'the icy fang/And churlish chiding of the winter's wind' are all too real and the inclement weather and lack of food nearly kill old Adam. The forest is full of savagery – later in the play Orlando saves Oliver from a snake and a lioness, and the Duke and his followers have to kill deer, 'poor dappled fools' in order to survive. The description of Jaques's grief at the lingering, bloody death of the deer shows up the decidely un-Arcadian qualities of forest life. Jaques extrapolates from this scene a vision of humanity that is anything but comic, and it is entirely appropriate that at the end of the play he should withdraw from the company of the human race, following the former duke into a religious order.

It has been pointed out by various commentators that these two plays are, far from being primarily romantic stories, actually plays about property relations. Discussing *As You Like It*, Louis Montrose suggests that Shakespeare makes a great issue of the laws of primogeniture, whereby the eldest son inherited from the father and then was supposed to take responsibility for the welfare of the younger sons, who became his dependents and adds that:

> Shakespeare's plays are thickly populated by subjects, sons, and younger brothers who are ambivalently bound to their lords, genitors and elder siblings – and by young women moving ambivalently between the lordships of father and husband. If this dramatic proliferation of patriarchs suggests that Shakespeare had a neurotic obsession, then it was one with a social context. To see father-figures everywhere in Shakespeare's plays is not a psychoanalytic anachronism, for Shakespeare's own contemporaries seem to have seen father-figures everywhere. . . . His plays explore the difficulty or impossibility of establishing or authenticating a self in a rigor-ously hierarchical and patriarchal society, a society in which

full social identity tends to be limited to propertied adult males who are heads of households.[3]

The situation of the two pairs of brothers in conflict in *As You Like It* is oppositional. Oliver treats his brother unjustly, and only in the forest does he come to recognise that his behaviour is 'unnatural'. This revelation occurs when Orlando follows the path of what Oliver describes as 'kindness' and 'nature' and saves his sleeping brother from wild beasts, hurting himself badly in the process. Oliver is immediately converted and so becomes a fit mate for Celia. In contrast, the older generation of brothers gives us a usurping younger brother who takes over his elder brother's dukedom unlawfully and who then cruelly abuses his newly found power. Only in the final moments of the play, when all the lovers have been united, does Jaques de Bois come with news of another unexpected conversion. Duke Frederick has gathered an army to drive out his older brother and his followers from the forest, but at the forest edge

> meeting with an old religious man,
> After some question with him, was converted
> Both from his enterprise and from the world;
> His crown bequeathing to his banished brother,
> And all their lands restored to them again
> That were with him exiled.
>
> (V. iv. 160–5)

In *A Midsummer Night's Dream*, miracles happen in the forest that bring lovers together. In *As You Like It*, the lovers are brought together by forces far more physical than magical. Miracles do still happen, this time it is the amazing conversion of the two bad brothers, thus ensuring that the property conflict will be resolved. Hymen may descend to bless the lovers, but Jaques de Bois is an equally welcome *deus ex machina*, who comes to bring the news of earthly, material well-being after the celebrations of the natural union brought about by love.

In *Twelfth Night* too, considerations of material and social status are important. The greatest contempt is reserved for Malvolio, the character who tries to move socially upward by marrying a woman from a class above him. In this play, the power relations are different, because Olivia is in control of her own household, and her relatives, Sir Toby and his friends are all her subordinates, since she has inherited everything after the death of her brother. Interestingly, in *Twelfth Night*, Sebastian and Viola, the twin outsiders, enter into the highest ranks of Illyrian society by marriage to Olivia and Duke Orsino respectively. What is denied to a member of Illyrian society from a lower rank is accessible to someone of equivalent rank from outside.

What *Twelfth Night* and *As You Like It* have most obviously in common is the narrative line that involves a woman disguising herself as a man for reasons of necessity and in that disguise both falling in love herself and becoming the object of another woman's love. Viola disguises herself as a man because she is shipwrecked in an unknown land and decides to survive by becoming page to Duke Orsino about whom she hears good reports. It is when Orsino decides to send her as his envoy to Olivia that the mistaken identity motif becomes most comic, and provides opportunity for some of the absurd scenes of wooing and avoidance:

OLIVIA: I prithee tell me what thou think'st of me.
VIOLA: That you do think you are not what you are.
OLIVIA: If I think so, I think the same of you.
VIOLA: Then think you right; I am not what I am.
OLIVIA: I would you were as I would have you be.

(III. i. 140–4)

In *As You Like It* the confusion of lovers reaches its peak in V. ii, when Silvius who loves Phoebe who thinks she is in love with Ganymede (Rosalind in disguise) meets the disguised Rosalind and Orlando, who is unaware that his young companion is really the woman he adores. The lovers recite a kind of litany to love, and only the audience can grasp the irony of what is being said:

PHOEBE: Good shepherd, tell this youth what 'tis to love.
SILVIUS: It is to be all made of sighs and tears;
    And so am I for Phoebe.
PHOEBE: And I for Ganymede.

ORLANDO: And I for Rosalind.
ROSALIND: And I for no woman.
(V. ii. 82–7)

Each time Rosalind's answer is the same: she does not love any woman, and so manages both to rebuff Phoebe who believes she is a man, while asserting her love for Orlando without his realising. It is a brilliant theatrical game and has entertained audiences for generations.

But behind the comic disguising and the absurd wooing sequences lies the reality of the unequal power held by men and women in Elizabethan society. Discussing her performance as Rosalind with the RSC, Juliet Stevenson believes that the final scene is 'emotionally contradictory'. Celia and Rosalind have defied authority and fled together into the forest; they have found their true loves and married them without seeking permission of anyone. As the play draws to a close, the women become increasingly silent:

> You can argue that Celia and Rosalind don't have to say anything more. . . . But you can argue, too, that they are silent for the same reason that they fell silent in Act I when the Court invaded their attic: that the patriarchy is reasserting itself. A male god dispenses marriage. . . . The god descends. The Duke takes over. And then the Court reasserts itself . . . the exiled Duke is restored to his position as the figure of ultimate authority and the hierarchies of the structured world re-emerge.[4]

The Duke takes over at the end of *Twelfth Night* too, rounding off the play with the promise of marriage between himself and Viola, so ensuring harmony between the two couples. In one respect this is a standard ending speech, but in another it is also a sign that patriarchal order has now been restored, the Duke is no longer the indolent lovesick man he was at the start of the play, he is now fully in control, while Olivia has been 'tamed' with a husband and the disguised Viola is about to become 'Orsino's mistress, and his fancy's queen'.

The comedy of female disguising was, of course, operating within a completely different set of signs on the Elizabethan stage. The sight of a skilful actress dressed as a boy may have delighted audiences from the eighteenth century onwards, but in Shakespeare's time what audiences saw was a boy player disguised as a woman disguised as a man, and so the jokes operated in another way entirely. It is difficult for contemporary minds to grasp all the implications of this style of performance; in twentieth-century western theatre there is no such convention in existence, and when we see Oriental theatre – Kathakali performers, for example – questions of gender tend not to be prioritised unless one is very familiar with the form, which most western spectators are not. The issue is further complicated by our inadequate understanding of the intense homoeroticism of the Elizabethan (and Renaissance) literary world in general. Having absorbed the puritanical values of the nineteenth century's attitude to homosexuality, it is difficult for many readers to accept the evidence in the Sonnets, for example, of Shakespeare's love for another man. Likewise, it is often conveniently forgotten that much of the humour in the situations of women disguised as men derived from the fact that those women were already young, sexually attractive men in female disguise. When Rosalind speaks her Epilogue, it is a very different speech if we know that the actor is male:

> If I were a woman I would kiss as many of you as had beards that pleased me, complexions that liked me, and breaths that I defied not

In her excellent book on women and drama in the age of Shakespeare, Lisa Jardine discusses the convention of cross-gender disguise:

> Wherever Shakespeare's female characters in the comedies draw attention to their own androgyny, I suggest that the resulting eroticism is to be associated with their maleness rather than with their femaleness. . . .
> I am arguing that in the drama the dependent role of the boy player doubles for the dependency which is woman's lot, creating a sensuality which is independent of the sex of the desired figure and which is particularly erotic where the sex

is confused (when boy player represents woman, disguised as a dependent boy).[5]

Jardine believes that the disguised boys are therefore sexually enticing because they are recognisably boys in female dress, and that the signs of femaleness within the plays are all directed towards that object.

This reading of Shakespeare makes a lot of sense. We have become accustomed in the twentieth century to think in terms of the great roles for women that Shakespeare wrote, simply because we always see women playing them. But Shakespeare wrote his female parts for men, and so as Jardine suggests, encoded into the portrayal of women are signs of maleness and of the kind of fantasy femaleness that we might find in the male transvestite today, where femaleness is perceived as glamorous clothing, jewellery and 'feminine' make-up. Although contemporary audiences may perceive Viola and Rosalind as strong, unconventional female characters, this reading is not one that Elizabethan audiences would have recognised; rather what they would have seen were sharp-witted androgynous figures who played games with the audience as much as with other characters in the plays about their sexual ambiguity.

The traditional focus on Rosalind and Viola as 'masculine' women has automatically cast Celia and Olivia into the subservient 'feminine' position. Rosalind is the principal female part in *As You Like It*, for which the leading actress is always cast, and Celia becomes a kind of sidekick. The text refers to Rosalind as taller than Celia, and once again the small size of actresses playing Celia has been used as a sign to reinforce Celia's fragility and femininity. Sinead Cusack, Celia in Terry Hands's 1982 RSC production, relates a significant anecdote about that director's view of the secondary position of Celia in the play. When she queried the fact that her costume was to be green, which would blend into the scenery and so marginalise her on stage, his reply was simply 'Don't be so stupid, Sinead. You are the set.'[6]

A reading of *As You Like It* that goes just one step beyond the tradition of romantic comedy with a jolly-hockey-sticks heroine reveals straight away how strong Celia is in comparison with Rosalind. It is Celia who stands up to her father, Celia who plans the flight to the forest, Celia who encourages Rosalind when she is downhearted, Celia who is the realist when Rosalind struggles to maintain her role of Ganymede. Celia's strength, like that of other Shakespearian heroines who critics have often, misguidedly, perceived as weak and 'feminine', for example Desdemona or Cordelia, derives from her assurance of her class position. When Rosalind despairs after her father's banishment, Celia encourages her. Celia's language is pithy, sharp and straight to the point; she does not waste time and does not suffer fools gladly. Even when she falls in love she does not beat about the bush, and it is not Celia but Rosalind who risks giving the game away when the two women are in disguise by displaying the tell-tale 'feminine' signs of weakness, as in this moment when Oliver tells them the story of Orlando's heroic fight with the lioness and Rosalind faints:

> CELIA: Why, how now, Ganymede! sweet Ganymede!
> OLIVER: Many will swoon when they do look on blood.
> CELIA: There is more in it. Cousin Ganymede!
> OLIVER: Look, he recovers.
> ROSALIND: I would I were at home.
> CELIA: We'll lead you thither.
> I pray you, will you take him by the arm?
>
> (IV. iii. 157–63)

Likewise, in *Twelfth Night*, Olivia is an aristocrat, and it is she who takes the lead, both in refusing Orsino and in wooing Viola. When Sebastian arrives in Illyria and she mistakes him for Viola, she organises a marriage at great speed. She brings a priest, tells Sebastian to go along with her and plight his troth 'That my most jealous and too doubtful soul/May live at peace' (IV. iii. 27–8). As they leave the stage to be married Olivia proclaims:

> Then lead the way, good father; and heavens so shine
> That they may fairly note this act of mine.
>
> (IV. iii. 34–5)

She has taken responsibility not only for arranging the marriage, but also for the implications of this action, since at this stage in the play she believes she is marrying a mere servant of the count. When the truth about Viola is finally revealed, it is significant that Viola falls into silence and the only female voice that can still be heard is the aristocratic voice of Olivia, trying to unravel the mystery of Malvolio and the letter.

The masculine disguise of Viola and Rosalind enables two women who are neither especially strong-willed (certainly less strong than either Olivia or Celia) nor established in society to survive in a hostile situation. The restoration of order at the end of the plays, the marriages and the return to the boundaries imposed by the accepted social hierarchy ensure that they can step out of their disguises thankfully and take up a place in the new order. Olivia will no longer be in charge of her estate, left her accidentally by the death of her brother, because she now has a husband, and Rosalind has not only a husband but an aristocratic father returned from exile.

The English convention of extolling the virtues of Rosalind and Viola and making them the centre of the action means that these two plays are generally handled on-stage in a fairly unadventurous manner. Designers vary the setting, but unlike the famous 1970 ‏production of *A Midsummer Night's Dream* by Peter Brook that radically altered readings and subsequent stagings of the play, *As You Like It* and *Twelfth Night* have not been accorded similar attention in English. Outside the conventions of English Shakespeare, however, the plays have undergone a radically different treatment. The 1981 Prague *Twelfth Night* directed by Jan Kačer in a translation by Alois Bejblik reduced the Viola–Olivia story to a farcical puppet play, and focused instead on what many traditionally have regarded as the 'sub-plot', the rise and fall of Malvolio. Taking a cue from the references to plague in the opening scene and the sadness of the final song, the Czech production brought out the ambiguities in Shakespeare's text, the sense of loss and disillusionment, interpreting the excessive speed with which people fall in love as a sign that the world outside Olivia and Orsino's palaces is a world of early death and disease. The play opened with a dumbshow, the burial of Olivia's brother, and the corpse of Malvolio was later carried in dumbshow and laid in the same space on the stage. Orsino appeared as a Renaissance prince, surrounded by androgynous courtiers, and Viola's false moustache and doublet and hose were the same uniform as that worn by Curio and Valentine.

The 1977 Berlin production by Peter Stein of *As You Like It* also brought out darker elements in the play, and the monumental staging of the first part emphasised the dangers and tensions inherent in courtly life. (All the scenes at Duke Frederick's court took place in the first half of the play, with the move to Arden in the second part.) Through the physical difference of the staging of these two disparate worlds, the point was made that the characters in the play are trapped by their own destinies; any flight to the forest is illusory, because the Arcadian ideal exists only in the imagination.

Innovative productions, such as these versions of *Twelfth Night* and *As You Like It*, in Czech and German respectively, bring out a central concern of both plays that is easily overlooked if we consider them simply as lighthearted love stories. Both plays are consciously theatrical, and time and again we are reminded of the artifice of theatre in all sort of ways. It was suggested in the previous chapter that the plays written at the turn of the six-teenth century were essentially metatheatrical, full of references to playing and constantly re-examining the idea of the play. Both *Twelfth Night* and *As You Like It* are about play-acting, about the assumption of disguise and the maintaining of roles despite circumstances that mitigate against such activity. 'So full of shapes is fancy', says Orsino in the opening scene of *Twelfth Night*, 'that it alone is high fantastical'. And in III. iv, after the mocking of the cross-gartered Malvolio, Fabian remarks 'if this were played upon a stage now, I could condemn it as improbable fiction' (III. iv. 134–5).

The fantastic setting of both plays points to the signedness of the stage itself, while the inconsistencies of time, place and character development stress the fact that the work of art creates its own universe and its own rules that may, in comparison with the laws of the external world, seem absurd. The desperate attempts of some critics to explain away these inconsistencies and to try and insist on 'realistic' characterisation is splendidly exemplified by the following passage:

The comedy of *Twelfth Night* is among the most perplexing of Shakespeare's plays to the stickler for accuracy of costume.

The period of action is undefined. The scene is laid in Illyria, whilst the names of the *dramatis personae* are a mixture of Spanish, Italian and English. The best mode of reconciling the discrepancies arising from so many conflicting circumstances appears to be the assumption, first, that Duke Orsino is a Venetian governor of Dalmatia, which was all of the ancient Illyria remaining under the dominion of the republic at the commencement of the seventeenth century, and that his attendants, Valentine, Curio, etc. as well as Olivia, Malvolio and Maria, are also Venetians; and secondly, that Sir Toby and Sir Andrew are English residents; the former a maternal uncle to Olivia – her father, a Venetian Count, having married Sir Toby's sister. If this is be allowed, and there is nothing that we can perceive in the play to prevent it, there is no impropriety in dressing the above-named characters in the Venetian and English costume of Shakespeare's own time, and the two sea-captains and Sebastian in the very picturesque habits of 'Chimariot, Illyrian and dark Suliote'. Viola might therefore, by assuming the *national* male dress, be more readily mistaken for her brother, as it is absurd to suppose that she could otherwise, by accident, light upon a facsimile of the suit he appears in; and any manifest difference, either in form or colour, would tend to destroy the illusion.[7]

That illusion can only be maintained by agreement with the audience, which both see through it and yet accept it at the same time. It is that collusion which gives exchanges such as the following their special comic effect: Rosalind's father and lover are discussing the boy Ganymede, remarking on how similar he is to Rosalind. The audience, of course, know who he really is, and are therefore in a position to laugh at the two men who have been deceived by a good piece of acting:

DUKE: I do remember in this shepherd boy
   Some lively touches of my daughter's favour.
ORLANDO: My lord, the first time that I ever saw him,
   Methought he was brother to your daughter.

                              (V. iv. 26–9)

As You Like It contains one of the best-known speeches on life as theatre in the whole of Shakespeare – Jaques's famous seven ages of man speech, beginning with the image of the world as a stage:

> All the world's a stage,
> And all the men and women merely players:
> They have their exits and their entrances;
> And one man in his time plays many parts,
> His acts being seven ages.
>
> (II. vii. 139–43)

Rosalind's epilogue again takes up the theatre–life metaphor, as the boy player confesses to his masculinity while at the same time affirming his status as a woman when playing a role: 'It is not the fashion to see the lady the epilogue', says this boy/woman but then goes on to joke about what he would do to the men if he were indeed a woman. The play has just ended, but the game goes on.

In *Twelfth Night* the figure who provides the link between the various strands in the plot is Feste, the clown, and significantly he is the only one designated as a player and paid for his services. (In *As You Like It* there is also a professional clown, Touchstone, another reminder of the theatricality of the world of the play.) Feste's song that concludes the play takes up the theme of the transience of the play world, but the dark hints of inclement weather ('Hey, ho, the wind and the rain') are not so much metaphysical as practical. What Feste's song says is: that's it, the play's over, we've done our best, but we are actors and we have to survive in the world outside 'and the rain it raineth every day'.

The confusion of interpretations of these plays has once again its roots in the conventions of naturalist characterisation that have so dominated Anglo-American dramatic criticism. The characterisation reading, fuelled by Stanislawskian acting theory, combines with the romantic comedy reading of *As You Like It* and *Twelfth Night* and results in two plays that have been perceived as being 'about' the tricks women will use to get their man. Rosalind and Viola are thus perceived as heroines, who use male clothing as part of their 'ruse' in much the same way as the heroines of Georgette Heyer's popular Regency love stories also used male disguise. But if we see the plays as being primarily 'about' characters, then inevitably there are all kinds of loose ends.

If, for example, we take the Orsino–Olivia–Viola line in *Twelfth Night* as being the centre of the play, then the Toby–Aguecheek–Maria–Malvolio line is relegated to the category of subplot, and it becomes problematic to explain why Feste and Malvolio introduce such dark notes into the general good humour. There is also the problem of Antonio, desperately fond of Sebastian and regarding himself as profoundly abused. He is left alone at the end of the play, unpartnered, a fact that has led Jan Kott among others to suggest that Antonio is actually in love with Sebastian, the 'girlish' boy. (The solitary position of another Antonio at the end of *The Merchant of Venice* is also an example of a man who sees the man he loves united in marriage with a woman.)

In *As You Like It*, there are constant threats of death – the forest is full of danger, the motif of deer-killing runs through the play, Jaques is a man well aware of the darker side not only of immediate circumstances but of human nature. The court is equally a place of danger; Duke Frederick usurps his brother's dukedom, then threatens Rosalind abruptly, with no prior warning. He is a tyrant who acts according to whim, and there can be no safety in a world ruled by such as he.

Obviously, it would be absurd to suggest that these two plays are tragic. The final resolution in both, even though it may leave a lot of questions unanswered, is a fairytale happy ending. In *As You Like It*, there are miraculous conversions, as wickedness suddenly turns to repentance, while in *Twelfth Night*, an identical twin appears to resolve the love-tangle. Such narrative devices restore a sense of good humour and remind us that the world of the play is a world of conscious artifice. But at the same time those darker elements need to be taken into account and not glossed over as irrelevant or secondary. The greatness of Shakespeare's comic vision is precisely that it is *not* lighthearted.

Twelfth Night and *As You Like It* invite questions about the linked but distinctive worlds of art (fancy) and life. When Viola, catching a reference to Sebastian, begins to hope that he might still be alive, she says to herself (and consequently, within the frame of the play, to the audience): 'Prove true, imagination, o prove true' (III. iv. 387). The irony is that such 'truth' can only occur within the fairytale fictitious world of the play. Outside, as Feste reminds us 'A great while ago the world begun . . . but that's all one, our play is done.' The play does not offer an escape from the world, it exists in a dialectical relationship to that world, just as the Forest of Arden exists in relation to the court.

9

The Rotten State: *Hamlet* and *Julius Caesar*

As the sixteenth century drew to a close, the end of the Tudor dynasty became inevitable. The Tudors had come to power in 1485, with the accession of Henry VII after the death of Richard III, and had been in control throughout the century, a period of massive religious upheaval, an age in which the map of the world had altered irrevocably with the eyes of European nations directed across the Atlantic Ocean. The death of Elizabeth in 1603 meant that the last of the Tudors would finally leave the stage, to be replaced by the son of her erstwhile rival, Mary Stuart. From the perspective of the twentieth century, the close of the sixteenth appears as a time of disillusionment and as a time of waiting. The high point of the Elizabethan age was long since over; the nation's economic crisis was intensified by the war in Ireland; the queen was old and tired, loosing her grip on a changing society. There is a sense of ending about many of the texts that date from this time. In so far as we read Shakespeare as an icon of his age, it is therefore significant that in the years on the cusp between the sixteenth and seventeenth centuries he wrote two very different kinds of tragedy that take up the themes of inheritance, rebellion, the pursuit of justice, and corruption in high places: *Julius Caesar* and *Hamlet*.

Julius Caesar dates from 1599 and is based quite closely on Sir Thomas North's translation of Plutarch's *Lives of the Noble Grecians and Romanes* (published in 1579), so closely that is is possible to make detailed comparisons between the two texts and to trace the ways in which Shakespeare developed the narrative for his own purposes. *Hamlet*, in complete contrast, has provided generations of critics with scope for debate, since alone of all of Shakespeare's plays it exists in three separate versions – the First Quarto, the Second Quarto and the First Folio – and appears to have as its source a range of rewritings of material that first appeared in a Latin history of the kings of Denmark, Saxo Grammaticus's *Danorum Regum Heroumque Historiae*, printed in Paris in 1514. The starting points of both *Julius Caesar* and *Hamlet* are therefore completely different, and the structure of the plays reflects that difference, even though there are some fundamental thematic links between them.

The origins of *Hamlet* lie in the convention of the revenge play, though as Muriel Bradbrook very succinctly puts it, that convention had undergone certain significant changes:

> The New Revenge writers were concerned with psychology rather than ethics; their comedy was bitter and fantastic in its ironies; their model was not Seneca but the witty Lucian's *Dialogue of the Dead*. The ducal Italy of the Renaissance was witty also in crime, especially the secret wittiness of the poisoner. . . . Hamlet is hemmed in by circumstances, by codes of duty in conflict with each other, prompted to his revenge 'By Heaven and Hell'.[1]

The traditional notion of the revenge play followed the pattern we have already seen in a play such as *Titus Andronicus*: terrible wrongs are committed, and are then avenged in bloodthirsty ways, following the old Biblical principle of an eye for an eye. The appeal of this kind of very basic morality to audiences is clear from the persistence of the tradition; the twentieth-century equivalent may be found first in the Hollywood western and then, more recently, in the vigilante movies starring revengers such as Charles Bronson. What is significantly different about *Hamlet*, however, is that although a wrong has been committed, and although the stage at the end of the play is littered

with corpses, including that of the protagonist, the process of
taking revenge is a very complex one. Hamlet is exhorted to
revenge by the ghost of his father – 'If thou hast nature in thee,
bear it not' (I. v. 81) – but he is also warned not to overstep the
mark by harming his mother:

> Let not the royal bed of Denmark be
> A couch for luxury and damned incest.
> But howsoever thou pursu'st this act,
> Taint not thy mind, nor let thy soul contrive
> Against thy mother aught: leave her to heaven
> And to those thorns that in her bosom lodge
> To prick and sting her.
>
> (I. v. 82–8)

Hamlet is therefore given a two-edged task – to avenge his
father but not to harm one of the two people who have taken
over the kingdom, for although Claudius may have been the sole
perpetrator of the actual murder of Old Hamlet, Gertrude has
married him and is ruling with him in apparent full agreement.
Hamlet's revenge is from the outset hamstrung, and through the
play he moves one step forward, then three steps backwards, un-
certain which way to move next, seeing himself 'be-netted round
with villainies' (V. ii. 29), missing vital opportunities, unable to
follow the dictum propounded by the unscrupulous Claudius
that 'revenge should have no bounds' (IV. vii. 127). Furthermore,
Hamlet is troubled with an inner pain even before the Ghost
confirms his worst suspicions about his uncle; he is in deepest
mourning for his dead father, bitter against his mother and in the
first scene in which he appears, he speaks the first of his great
soliloquies: 'Oh that this too too sullied flesh would melt', expressing a feeling of angst and disillusionment that so captured
the Romantic imagination and has held audiences ever since:

> How weary, stale, flat and unprofitable
> Seem to me all the uses of this world!
> Fie on't, ah fie, 'tis an unweeded garden
> That grows to seed.
>
> (I. ii. 133–6)

The popularity of Hamlet from the eighteenth century onwards is undeniable. 'The king of all plays . . . the jewel in the crown which honours the artist more than him who wears it . . . the ornament of all stages, diamond of all libraries' is how Ulrich Bräker described *Hamlet* in 1780,[2] while Coleridge noted that *Hamlet* had been 'the darling of every country in which the literature of England has been fostered'.[3] The figure of Hamlet has passed into mythology, and the image of the student prince, dressed in black, tormented by the angst of human existence, desperate to act and yet unable to do so has become an instantly recognisable archetype. When pantomime comedians appear wearing black doublet and hose and carrying a skull, they immediately signal 'Hamlet' to an audience. Millions of people who have never read the play nor know the plot, can nevertheless recognise Hamlet on the basis of certain crucial archetypal signs. The play offers a world-vision, and its language has a decisive place in Western cultural history.

If Hamlet is an archetypal figure for post-Enlightenment readers onwards, then the story of the assassination of Julius Caesar by Brutus, Cassius and their fellow conspirators has stirred the imaginations of readers and writers in previous centuries.

In his *Divine Comedy,* Dante placed Brutus and Cassius down in the lowest depths of hell, where they are eternally gnawed in the very jaws of the devil, along with the greatest sinner of all time, Judas Iscariot. Brutus and Cassius were, for the medieval mind, icons of treachery: just as Judas betrayed the heavenly king, so they betrayed their earthly ruler, Caesar. Given Shakespeare's fascination with the problem of revolt against an anointed monarch in his histories, it is not surprising that he would turn to a Roman source that took up the same theme, but what is significant about his treatment of the story is his portrayal of Brutus, who has a lot in common with Hamlet.

From his first appearance, Brutus, like Hamlet, is troubled:

> I am not gamesome: I do lack some part
> Of that quick spirit that is in Antony.
> . . . .
> Vexed I am
> Of late with passions of some difference,

Conceptions only proper to myself,
Which give some soil, perhaps, to my behaviours.
(I. ii. 28–9; 39–42)

At first resistent to the idea, Brutus comes to believe that the
death of Caesar is necessary to ensure the health of the state. He
joins the conspiracy, though refuses to go along with the second
proposition to kill Mark Antony: 'Let us be sacrificers, but not
butchers, Caius' (II. i. 166). True to his word, he joins in the
killing of Caesar, and then, idealistic revolutionary that he is,
proclaims the new freedom:

Stoop, Romans, stoop,
And let us bathe our hands in Caesar's blood
Up to the elbows and besmear our swords.
Then walk we forth, even to the market-place,
And waving our red weapons o'er our heads
Let's all cry, 'Peace, freedom, and liberty!'
(III. i. 105–10)

This is the pivotal point in the play; Brutus's refusal to have
Antony killed and his permission to allow Antony to speak at
Caesar's funeral seals his own doom; the Machiavellian Antony
moves the crowd to tears, persuading them that Caesar has been
wrongfully murdered, and Brutus's dreams of a new, liberal
order are destroyed. From here onwards it is a steady movement
towards death; on the night before the battle of Philippi, the
ghost of Caesar appears to Brutus in his tent, declaring itself to
be his evil spirit, while Cassius commits suicide, declaring
'Caesar, thou art revenged' (V. iii. 45) The conspirators die, while
the new generation of hard men, personified in the characters of
Antony and Octavius, take over the state.

Octavius orders Brutus to be buried with full military
honours, commanding that his body be treated with all respect,
as befits the man described by Antony as 'the noblest Roman of
them all' (V. v. 68). *Hamlet* ends on precisely the same conventional note, with Fortinbras ordering four captains to 'bear
Hamlet like a soldier to the stage' (V. ii. 390). Brutus's decision
to act, and to kill the man whom he feared would become a
tyrant, and Hamlet's inability to act and to kill the man he knew

as a tyrant, both lead to the same result: the state is taken over by someone possibly even more unscrupulous, and the dead, idealistic hero is buried with full military honours. In the case of Brutus this is appropriate; it is singularly inappropriate for Hamlet, the scholar, who had interrupted his studies in Wittenberg and whose attempt to return to university was blocked by Claudius early in the action of the play.

Fortinbras, the Norwegian prince, is a counterpart to Hamlet, and is sometimes perceived as Hamlet's *alter ego*. In I. i, Horatio describes how Fortinbras is seeking to avenge his father, killed by Old Hamlet, and to take back the lands lost to Denmark by his father. Fortinbras is a military hero, an active avenger. Like Hamlet, he believes the 'state to be disjoint' (I. ii. 20) and brings an army to assert his claim. While Hamlet agonises over the question of what lies beyond death, and whether he should kill Claudius while the king is at prayer, so enabling him to die in a state of grace, Fortinbras moves in a linear way towards his goal. As Hamlet lies dying, he recognises that Fortinbras's accession is inevitable:

> But I do prophesy th'election lights
> On Fortinbras. He has my dying voice.
> So tell him, with th'occurrents, more and less,
> Which have solicited – the rest is silence.
>   (V. ii. 355–8)

Hamlet dies before he can finish his sentence, and so the mystery of what he might have said dies with him. Opinion is sharply divided as to what Fortinbras signifies here: is he a militaristic tyrant who storms into the castle and finds unexpectedly that the dying prince has handed over the kingdom without any resistance, or is he a noble prince in his own right who merits the trust that Hamlet places in him? Critics and directors split on this issue, but what does seem clear is that however we see Fortinbras, he is an outsider, and although he may be a prince and a military commander, he is not a Dane. Hamlet has handed over the kingdom into the hands of the son of his father's enemy, and Denmark is destined to belong in the future to Norway.

In his essay on *Hamlet*, Grigori Kosintsev, the Soviet director, suggests that the play depicts the passing of the old order and the coming of the new, counter-Reformation ideology:

> From the middle of the sixteenth century, reaction gradually became triumphant everywhere. Old forms of oppression were replaced not by free associations of wise citizens but by an even crueller slavery. Many titans of the Renaissance had come to learn how 'Wittenberg' yielded to 'Elsinore'.
>
> Hamlet was the expression of more than the personal tragedy of the princely student; it was also the historied tragedy of humanism, the tragedy of those who gave too much swing to their wit. The time came when thought led to suffering.[4]

Fortinbras represents the new order, as do Antony and Octavius when they sit round a table determining quite dispassionately who shall die. They are all representatives of an opportunistic materialism, and can back up their demands with military strength. It is not surprising that a number of post-1945 productions of *Julius Caesar* and of *Hamlet* have encoded Nazi symbolism into the staging, for the problem of totalitarianism runs through both plays. Brutus and Hamlet are, in their different ways, both idealists, and for both expediency is never the first thought in their minds. Their deaths are tragic, but at the same time, inevitable, for it is clear in both plays that their views are out of line with the dynamic forces around them.

Both plays focus very much on the conflict in Brutus and in Hamlet between their sense of themselves in public and their private needs. The relationship between Hamlet and Ophelia, which critics have extensively discussed, has a parallel in the relationship between Brutus and Portia. Both women die: Ophelia, driven mad, falls into the water and is drowned; Portia chokes herself by swallowing hot coals. The symbolism of these two deaths is striking: in both cases the woman is marginal to the man she loves, and in both cases is driven by her desperation to seek her own death, a death that involves choking. Gertrude's account of Ophelia's death describes how she sang as she lay in the stream until pulled under 'from her melodius lay/To muddy death' (IV. vii. 182–3): Brutus tells Cassius that Portia also lost her reason: 'she fell distract / And, her attendants absent, swallowed fire' (IV. iii. 155–6). Excluded from the confidence of their menfolk, relegated to silence, both die horribly, choked in the confused world of madness. After her death, Hamlet proclaims his great love for Ophelia, but his earlier rejection of her, combined with his killing of her father, Polonius, have combined to make her lose her reason. Likewise, Portia is unable to endure absence from Brutus, or to accept the destruction of his ideals with the new-found power of Octavius and Antony. Hamlet and Brutus may claim to have loved Ophelia and Portia respectively, but they are responsible for their deaths nevertheless.

Women are peripheral in both *Hamlet* and *Julius Caesar*, they have no place in the world outside the home and family, and are at the mercy of the powerful males who can move between the domestic and the public spheres with ease. Even Gertrude, the queen, has minimal power. It is her husband who gives the orders, and she is tormented by what she believes to be the tangible evidence of her son's madness. Her death, which happens by mistake, when she drinks the poison intended for Hamlet, is an ignoble one. '[T]he King's to blame', says Laertes, when Gertrude falls dead and he realises that the poison is killing him also. Gertrude is no Lady Macbeth, no Goneril or Regan, merely a wife and mother, an appendage, in the same way as poor Calpurnia is an appendage to Caesar, a barren woman afflicted by disturbing dreams of his impending death, but whose advice is ignored.

Both *Julius Caesar* and *Hamlet* end with what David Leverenz has called 'a mindless sequence of ritual male duties'.[5] The militaristic rite that concludes both plays emphasises the imposition of the new order; the self-doubt, the moral questioning, the ethical debate propounded by Hamlet and Brutus have no place in a world ruled by such men as Fortinbras and Octavius. But although the conclusion to the two plays is similar, the path that leads to such an ending moves through very different terrain. The emphasis in *Hamlet* is on the protagonist himself, on his inner turmoil and outward interaction with the surrounding court; in *Julius Caesar* the contrast is principally between the private world of the group of men in power (or desirous to be in power) and the public world of those who are subject to them.

The opening scene of *Julius Caesar* introduces that public

world, and it is possible to argue that 'the people' are virtually a collective character in this play. Certainly the people appear regularly, and although Casca may deride them as 'the common herd', the 'the rabblement', 'the rag-tag people', their response to the speeches of Brutus and Antony determines the fate of both men. Antony knows how to manipulate the people, he has learned the art of appealing to their secret fears and desires, whilst Brutus has no sense of what the people might want, other than what he expects of them. In this respect, the difference between the approach of Brutus and Antony is the difference between an idealist and a politician; Brutus is indeed an honourable man, but he does not know how to use his honourable reputation, and so the scheming Antony is able to undermine his authority with ease.

The play opens with Flavius and Marullus, two tribunes, urging the people not to celebrate Caesar's triumph: 'You blocks, you stones, you worst than senseless things!' (I. i. 38) cries Marullus, reminding the populace that Caesar is responsible for the deposition and death of Pompey, their former hero. The two men never reappear in the play, and later we learn that they have been put to death for tearing the decorations down from Caesar's statues. What this opening sequence does, therefore, is establish the fickleness of the people, and also the futility of idealistic gestures. Flavius and Marullus try to speak to the crowd, but are ignored: 'See where their basest metal be not moved' (I. i. 60) and so their revolution is doomed from its outset. To succeed in the world of this play, a man must be astute, unscrupulous and manipulative, and then back up his tactical politicking with military strength. Caesar, although we see little of him, has come to power in this way, and although Cassius resents the hypocrisy that gives 'a man of such feeble temper' control over all Rome, he recognises that it is Caesar's own skill, not some innate virtue that has placed him over all of them:

Why, man, he doth bestride the narrow world
Like a Colossus, and we petty men
Walk under his huge legs and peep about
To find ourselves dishonourable graves.
Men at some times are masters of their fates:

> The fault, dear Brutus, is not in our stars
> But in ourselves, that we are underlings.
>   (I. ii. 135–41)

That same drive for power, combined with a lack of scruples that leads him to murder his own brother, has brought Claudius to power in Denmark, though, unlike Caesar, we know next to nothing about his reputation outside the court. We hear Hamlet's comparison of his uncle with his father, but this remains on a personal level. Indeed, the absence of the people in *Hamlet* is quite striking, considering that King Claudius has taken over the throne following the death of his brother despite the presence of a son and heir. Hamlet himself is far more concerned with his uncle's incest than with his own lost throne, and the murder of Gonzago, the play staged at Hamlet's insistence by the Players, focuses on the relationship between the guilty queen and her fratricidal lover. The action of *Hamlet* takes place within the claustrophobic atmosphere of the court, and the world outside is represented by the graveyard or by accounts of the military victories of Fortinbras.

The 1980 production of *Hamlet* by Footsbarn, the travelling company of clowns, succeeded magnificently in bringing out the sense of suffocation in the play. The company chose deliberately to cut all Hamlet's great speeches, thereby restoring to the play a sense of excitement that is frequently missing in productions where the soliloquies stand out like arias in an opera. The play was staged in the round, and throughout the action, masked clowns continually spied on anyone who happened to be in the playing area. This comic device stressed the conspiratorial feeling generated by the play, for throughout the action of *Hamlet*, people spy constantly on one another – Polonius and Claudius spy on Hamlet and Ophelia, Polonius meets his end spying on Hamlet and Gertrude, Hamlet spies on Claudius, Rosencrantz and Guildenstern spy on Hamlet and so forth. The play is full of sequences in which one character plots against another or in which reports of what someone is supposed to have said are transmitted to someone else. Even the Ghost lurks within the castle, intervening at the crucial moment when Hamlet confronts his mother in her chamber.

Only once does it seem as though the closed world of the

court is about to be broken: maddened by news of his father's death, Laertes assembles a crowd of supporters and storms the castle. Claudius orders his mercenaries to guard the door, but a messenger arrives with news of the rebellion:

> Laertes in a riotous head,
> O'erbears your officers. The rabble call him lord,
> And, as the world were now but to begin,
> Antiquity forgot, custom not known,
> The ratifiers and props of every word,
> They cry 'Choose we! Laertes shall be king!'
> Caps, hands and tongues applaud it to the clouds:
> 'Laertes shall be king! Laertes king!'
>
> (IV. v. 100–7)

A constant question that is never answered in *Hamlet* is why the Danes have apparently consented to the accession of a brother over the claim of a son, and why they would support the crowning of a man who is not even a member of the nobility instead of the prince. The right of primogeniture is clearly the source of Fortinbras's actions, and at the end of the play Hamlet is deemed to be Claudius's successor when he confers the right to the crown onto Fortinbras. Yet at no point does there appear to be any common support for Hamlet's claim to the throne; there is indeed something so rotten in the state of Denmark that basic patterns of inheritance can be completely disregarded. Claudius refers to Hamlet as 'our chiefest courtier, cousin, and our son' (I. ii. 117). No hint is never made that Hamlet might be his father's rightful successor.

Hamlet and *Julius Caesar* treat similar issues, but from very different perspectives. The closed world of the court in *Hamlet* is emphasised by the imagery of rankness and decay, and the graveyard becomes emblematic of the world. Hamlet's bitter rhyme is a parable:

> Imperious Caesar, dead and turned to clay,
> Might stop a hole to keep the wind away.
> O, that that earth which kept the world in awe
> Should patch a wall t'expel the winter's flaw!
>
> (V. i. 221–4)

Nothing is certain in this corrupt, confused world. Laws are changed at will, princes are deposed without a murmur, wives remarry their brothers-in-law, the dead return to speak to the living. Yet even the realm of the dead fuels uncertainty; the Ghost tells Hamlet that the afterworld is a prison-house of which he is forbidden to speak, but hints that the pains he is suffering, in what appears to be purgatory, are unspeakable. Hamlet himself reflects on what death means, on the 'dread of something after death' (III. i. 78). The court of Denmark and the afterworld appear, to Hamlet, to be as bleak and full of anguish as the graveyard where he sees the skull of his childhood playmate, the jester Yorick.

The absence of the people in *Hamlet* focuses attention on the court and in particular on the inner world of Hamlet's own mind. Shakespeare has once again used the familiar theme of just and unjust rule, but has concentrated this time on the inner struggle of the would-be avenger. Although we have glimpses into Claudius's mind also, the focus remains on Hamlet, and this is in contrast to the pattern established in those history plays that deal with similar themes.

It is the question of the afterworld that marks most sharply the difference between *Julius Caesar* and *Hamlet*. In his version of one of the great betrayal stories of the medieval world, Shakespeare gives us an heroic Brutus, a man who despises violence but is not afraid to strike a blow; a man who can quietly accept the apparition of his victim as a sign of his own impending death and who can then go to that death with stoicism. Ghosts and graves hold no terrors for Brutus, and as he runs on his sword in his final suicidal gesture, his last words are:

> Caesar, now be still,
> I killed not thee with half so good a will.
> (V. v. 49–50)

The linearity of the structure of *Julius Caesar* owes a great deal to Plutarch, but it is also clear that Shakespeare offers us the story of Brutus's tragic dilemma in very straightforward terms, as the crisis of a good man caught between differing ideologies. The highly complex structure of *Hamlet* reflects the complexity of the issues tackled within the play as much as it reflects the

multifarious nature of Shakespeare's sources, and in consequence it is a work that has been interpreted in very different
ways by successive generations of audiences and readers.

Goethe offered an image of Hamlet as a contemporary of
young Werther, a pure nature unable to endure the burden
placed upon his shoulders, typifying the anxiety of a young
intellectual at the start of the Age of Revolutions. *Fin-de-siècle*
writers saw Hamlet as a drama of death; existentialists saw
Hamlet as the outsider, unable to free himself by the liberating
act of killing Claudius, unlike Sartre's Oreste who, despite his
fears of future punishment, summoned up the courage to
murder his mother Clytemnestre. Approaching *Hamlet* today, all
these different readings have become part of our inheritance, and
because of the great symbolic power of the Prince of Denmark it
is easy to move away from the play's starting point in the world
at the end of close of the sixteenth century.

Voltaire was instrumental in the one great shift in how we
have come to perceive *Hamlet*, for it was Voltaire who moved the
focus away from conscience as religious crisis, to conscience
as the dilemma of the individual mind, in keeping with the
ideology of the Age of Reason. Yet many of the unanswered
questions raised in the play can only be dealt with if we go back
to the vexed question of Christian consciousness and the interaction between this world and the next. 'Angels and ministers of
grace defend us!' prays Hamlet, when he first sees the Ghost,
and the Ghost tells Hamlet plainly that he resides in a place of
utter horror and torment until the crimes he committed in life are
purged. Hamlet's fear of 'The undiscovered country, from whose
bourn/No traveller returns' (III. i. 79–80) is voiced in the 'To be
or not to be' soliloquy, where he also notes that 'conscience does
make cowards of us all'. Conscience here is not so much a sense
of guilt, but rather a sense of awareness, a moral code that
constrains the individual from acting in ways that offend against
a moral order. Hamlet shares with Brutus a powerful inner
feeling of moral strength; the difference between them is that
Brutus's morality is part of a world-view that sees earthly
existence as all; Hamlet's morality, however, is located firmly in
a Christian world, but one in which the centrality of a single
church had been destroyed. The Ghost may refer to the purging
fires, but the Reformation had abolished Purgatory, in favour of

a straight binary split between heavan and hell. Hamlet typifies the crisis of the man of the northern Renaissance, the man who studied at Wittenberg, the university where both Luther and Melanchthon taught, and the deliberate reference to Wittenberg in I. ii –when Claudius informs Hamlet that his wish to return to university 'is most retrograde to our desire' – would have been a clear signal to Elizabethan audiences of Hamlet's religious persuasion. Likewise, in the same scene, Laertes pleads to be allowed to return to France, and the contrast between Protestant Germany and Catholic France presages the conflict of the two young men that ends in both their deaths.

Julius Caesar works on a balance between different elements, between the public, the private and, in the scene before Phillipi, the supernatural world. Wolfgang Clemen argues that it is possible to distinguish clear points of climax in the action of the play:

> *Julius Caesar* is a political play. Groups are formed and jeopardized, plans are considered and rejected, guesses about the future actions of partners and opponents are hazarded, mistrust and fear, trust and miscalculations alternate with one another and time and again direct the attention of the characters and of the audiences to the future.[6]

This pattern, he suggests, does not happen in *Hamlet*, despite the similarity of much of the thematic material. There is no clear climax, instead there are devices that create suspense and make the play function on several levels simultaneously. This interpretation is helpful, and it is as though *Julius Caesar* and *Hamlet* represent two different ways of discussing the same issue: the breaking-up of the old order and the coming of a new order that still lacks any definable shape. No one knows, at the end of either play, what the new hard men in control will bring to the troubled states of Rome and Denmark.

The political 'message' of both plays is conveyed quite specifically through the metaphor of performance. In *Julius Caesar*, the speeches at Caesar's funeral exemplify the difference between 'life' and 'theatre'. Brutus speaks from the heart, he is honest and straightforward, using prose to express his forthright views:

> Who is here so base that would be a bondman? If any, speak,
> for him have I offended. Who is here so rude that would not
> be a Roman? If any, speak, for him have I offended. Who is
> here so vile that will not love his country? If any, speak, for
> him have I offended. I pause for a reply.   (III. ii. 25–9)

This kind of crude rhetoric naturally elicits a response of 'None,
Brutus, none' from the crowd, and Brutus proceeds to declare
bluntly 'Then none have I offended'. But Antony's use of language is altogether different. Using similar rhetorical figures to
Brutus, using the device of the question, but this time not
eliciting an answer, Antony moves the people to violence against
Brutus and his comrades. The mistake that Brutus makes is the
mistake of the bad actor: to speak directly to the crowd, trying
to bring them into his performance, ignoring the gap between
stage and audience. Antony, on the other hand, gives them the
illusion of being at one with him, but maintains the space
between performer and public. He is a master of the art of stage
illusion, and ironically illusion can seem more real than reality
itself. This is something that Hamlet understands, and in his
famous question 'What's Hecuba to him, or he to Hecuba,/That
he should weep for her' (II. ii. 566–7) he acknowledges that
theatre can move an emotional response more than real life.
When he chooses to stage a play about the murder of a king by
his brother, he is explicit about his intentions: 'The play's the
thing/Wherein I'll catch the conscience of the King' (II. ii.
614–15). And so powerful is the playing of *The Mousetrap* that
Claudius orders the play interrupted, for he cannot watch a
fictitious version of the crime he has not shrunk from committing
in real life.

The actors' fictitious representation disturbs Claudius, though
he himself is a master of the art of dissimulation. Plotting with
Laertes to kill Hamlet on his return from England, Claudius says:

> Let's think further of this
> Weigh what convenience both of time and means
> May fit us to our shape. If this should fail,
> And that our drift look through our bad performance,
> 'Twere better not essay'd.
>
> (IV. vii. 147–51)

Claudius is playing a role throughout, concealing the crime that has brought him to power, seeking to hide his evil intentions. Like Mark Antony, he is a man who has studied Machiavelli, who has learned the art of honeying the nastiest of sties. Ironically, when the audience sees his mask drop in III. iii as he tries to pray, Hamlet, who is watching, is incapable of distinguishing performance from reality, and holds back from killing him because he believes that Claudius is genuinely in touch with God at that moment.

Hamlet's own play-acting is less consistent, less immediately apparent. Claudius schemes, and kills, and strives to maintain his public image, while Hamlet veers between explosions of what appear to be madness and bleak despair. There are aspects of Hamlet that recall Prince Henry, the young man locked in combat with his father, and playing out the role of madcap while it served him to do so. In IV. iv Hamlet abruptly changes direction, dropping the role of mad prince, and in his 'How all occasions do inform against me' soliloquy he seems finally to take on the role of young avenger:

> O, from this time forth
> My thoughts be bloody or be nothing worth.
> (IV. iv. 64–5)

The play-acting is over; from this time onwards Hamlet is a changed man, grieving over the dead Ophelia, fighting Laertes, finally meeting his death with stoicism and courage. Significantly, in V ii, when he tells Horatio about the journey to England and his discovery of the treachery of Rosencrantz and Guildenstern, he does so through the metaphor of the play:

> Being thus benetted round with villainies –
> Ere I could make a prologue to my brains,
> They had begun the play – I sat me down,
> Devis'd a new commission, wrote it fair –
> I once did hold it, as our statists do,
> A baseness to write fair, and labour'd much
> How to forget that learning, but, sir, now
> It did me yeoman's service.
> (V. ii. 29–36)

Hamlet's letter sends Rosencrantz and Guildenstern to their
deaths, leaving him free to return to Denmark to exact his
revenge at last. 'Why, what a king is this!' comments Horatio in
response to Hamlet's account of his English journey, and in this
scene between the two men, two major threads running through
the play are pulled together. Horatio's phrase equates kingliness
with learning to command and control; Hamlet is a king because
he has learned to play the part of kings and has cleverly forged
the document that dooms Rosencrantz and Guildenstern. Playing a role and asserting power are here equated, as they are
again in Fortinbras's instructions for Hamlet's funeral:

> Let four captains
> Bear Hamlet like a soldier to the stage,
> For he was likely, had he been put on,
> To have prov'd most royally.
> (V. ii. 404–7)

Fortinbras's view is that had Hamlet, the actor/prince, ever
made his stage début, he would have been good in the part. But
Hamlet dies before he has learned fully how to take hold of the
reins of power, and like Brutus, the noblest Roman of them all,
has ambiguous feelings about the very nature of kingship. He is
given a military funeral, but Horatio's farewell – 'Good night,
sweet prince/And flights of angels sing thee to thy rest' – is far
more appropriate.

The state, in both *Hamlet* and *Julius Caesar*, is afflicted with a
disease; it is rotting away in the grip of tyrants and demagogues,
unscrupulous politicians and a fickle public. Brutus and Hamlet
are out of place in such a context, and though both commit acts
of violence, it is against the principles they each express. The
stoic idealist who sees his dreams of freedom destroyed by a
master manipulator, and the scholar whose dreams of study are
disturbed by an unquiet spirit urging him to avenge a murder,
are both portrayed as men seeking honesty in a world of
deception. The metaphor of the world as theatre, which
Shakespeare used so frequently, is especially powerful in relation
to these two plays. Is it not monstrous, says Hamlet, reflecting

on the skill of the Players to create emotion out of 'conceit', that an actor who feels no pain can nevertheless shape a impression of pain that moves a man to tears? In art, such a talent is put to a specific use, but in the arena of politics, as when Antony exhorts the crowd to listen with 'If you have tears, prepare to shed them now', such a talent is dangerous in the extreme.

10
The Fairytale in Crisis: *Much Ado About Nothing*, *Troilus and Cressida* and *All's Well That Ends Well*

Queen Elizabeth died in March 1603 in her seventieth year. The execution of Essex in 1601 had caused her considerable grief, as had the death of several cherished friends. Shortly before she died, Sir John Harington commented on the decline of her physical and mental powers in a letter to his wife: 'Our dear Queen doth now bear show of human infirmity.'[1] Members of her court had been in secret contact with James VI in Scotland, waiting in Edinburgh for the word to move southwards and assume the throne; as the queen grew weaker, anticipation of her dying increased. The new king would unite Scotland with England, the new century would take the fortunes of the nation in very different directions.

For Shakespeare, the Queen's death had immediate repercussions. The theatres were closed shortly before her death on 24 March for a period of mourning. They had barely time to reopen, when a severe outbreak of plague closed them again, this time until the spring of 1604. But James declared his support for theatre, despite the ban on playing, by creating the company

154

known as the King's Men, out of the former Chamberlain's men. William Shakespeare was one of the names mentioned in the letters patent, which licensed the company to:

> freely use and exercise the arte and faculty of playing Comedies, Tragedies, histories, Enterludes, moralls, pastoralls, Stage-plaies, and Such others like as they have alreadie studied or hereafter shall use or studie . . . [and] to shewe and exercise publiquely to their best Commoditie, when the infection of the plague shall decrease, as well within theire nowe usual howse called the Globe within our County of Surrey, as alsoe within the liberties and freedome of anie other Cittie, universitie, towne, or Borough whatsoever within our said Realmes and domynions.[2]

Critics have often pointed out that after 1604, Shakespeare's work moved into new dimensions; the great tragedies from *Othello* onwards were all written after this date, and he moved away from romantic comedies, creating instead that cluster of plays often termed 'pastoral'. Biographical critics have sometimes tried to link problems in Shakespeare's life with the death of the old queen, noting an increasing concern in Shakespeare's plays with images of death and decay – the rottenness of the state of Denmark being paralleled to the rottenness of Shakespeare's own country, still ruled by an ageing, decrepit monarch. If Shakespeare had been close to Southampton and to Essex, then the failure of the Essex rebellion, the execution of Essex himself and the incarceration of Southampton must have fuelled feelings of discontent. The execution of Essex had taken place in 1601, the year in which Shakespeare's father had died. It is therefore probably not unfair to speculate on Shakespeare's state of mind at the beginning of the new century, on the basis of what we know about his circumstances and also what we can deduce from the plays written around this time.

After *Hamlet*, Shakespeare wrote the three plays that have come to be termed the 'problem' plays: *Troilus and Cressida*, *All's Well That Ends Well* and, after 1604, *Measure for Measure*. The 'problem' of these plays refers as much to the subject matter as to the way in which the plays are structured, for all three offer glimpses of the darker side of human nature, unredeemed by any tragic grandeur. For the purposes of this book, *Measure for Measure* will be considered as belonging to the plays of James's reign, though obviously it is somewhat spurious to separate one writer's artistic production neatly according to the dates of the death and accession of monarchs. More appropriately, however, it can be argued that *Measure for Measure* has stylistic features in common with some of the tragedies, while the other two 'problem' plays are still closely linked to the plays written at the end of the 1590s. Most particularly, *Troilus and Cressida* and *All's Well That Ends Well* share a common link with the slightly earlier *Much Ado About Nothing* (printed in 1600 but probably written at the end of 1598), for all three deal with the subject of faithfulness in love and the significance of the marriage contract.

Much Ado About Nothing is usually considered to be a romantic comedy and so is discussed together with *As You Like It* and *Twelfth Night*, to which it is closest in terms of date of writing. Like the games played by Rosalind and Orlando, or Viola and Olivia, the verbal battles between Beatrice (a shrew-like figure but far less bitter than Katharina) and Benedick (a bluff military man like Petruchio, who turns himself into a lover rather than into a wife-tamer) have delighted audiences for centuries. A poem of 1640 says

> Let but Beatrice
> And Benedick be seen, lo in a trice
> The Cockpit, galleries, boxes, all are full.[3]

Unlike Katharina and Petruchio, Beatrice and Benedick are more equally matched; both claim to despise one another:

> BEATRICE: I wonder that you will still be talking, Signor Benedick, nobody marks you.
> BENDICK: What, my dear Lady Disdain! Are you yet living?
> BEATRICE: Is it possible Disdain should die, while she hath such meet food to feed it, as Signor Benedick?
> (I. i. 115–20)

Even at the conclusion of the play, when they acknowledge that they are in love with one another, this game continues:

BENDICK: Come, I will have thee, but by this light I take thee
   for pity.
BEATRICE: I would not deny you, but by this good day, I yield
   upon great persuasion, and partly to save your life, for I
   was told you were in a consumption.

(V. iv. 94-100)

Despite the enjoyment generated by watching two adversaries
fall in love with one another, as Jean Howard has argued in a
very perceptive essay on the politics of gender and rank in *Much
Ado About Nothing*, Beatrice and Benedick are manoeuvred into
love by the machinations of Don Pedro, who stages the scenes
where each 'finds out about' the apparent lovesickness of the
other.[4] They both believe Don Pedro's playlets and so begin a
process of self-questioning that ultimately makes them declare
their love for one another. What we see taking place is not only
a process of revelation for two people who are already drawn to
one another, it is also a process of manipulation by the figure
who represents authority.

Moreover, despite the good humour of the Beatrice–Benedick
plot, there is another much darker strand running through the
play; Don Pedro's corrupt brother, John, devises a scheme to
harm his brother. Don Pedro's favourite, Claudio, is to marry
Hero, Beatrice's sister. John stages a playlet of his own, this time
designed not to bring lovers together but to drive them apart. He
and his associates stage a scene that leads Don Pedro and
Claudio to believe that Hero has been entertaining a lover in her
bedroom, having first planted the idea of Hero's unfaithfulness
in their minds. When Hero comes to be married, Claudio
publicly repudiates her: 'Give not this rotten orange to your
friend' (IV. i. 33). The innocent bride is calumnied and there
appears to be no redress.

In the end, the situation is saved by the intervention of the
clowns, Dogberry and his watchmen who expose John. Mean-
while, as punishment, Claudio and Don Pedro have been led to
believe that Hero is dead, and Claudio as penance agrees to
marry an unknown woman, that Leonato claims is his niece, 'a
copy of my child that's dead'. In true fairytale tradition, the
unknown woman turns out to be Hero herself, who had been

alive all the time and the play ends with the double wedding of
Beatrice and Benedick, and Claudio and Hero.

The trial of Hero is particularly unpleasant in this play, not
only because she is innocent, but also because she is so completely unaware of what is going on. Don Pedro and Claudio are
men of high social status, and when they call her a whore, their
word is believed by everyone except Hero's sister, Beatrice and
the Friar. The visible signs of innocence in Hero's face that
convince the Friar straight away are not noticed by Claudio; he
believes only the evidence of what he thought he saw at Hero's
bedroom window, and that scene was already prejudicated by
John's story of Hero's unchastity. The clown scenes and the final
restoration cannot take away the taste of ashes left by the re-
pudiation scene; even the games of Beatrice and Benedick are
tainted by it, as she urges him to kill Claudio and he agrees to
challenge him, not necessarily because he believes in Hero's
innocence but because Beatrice does.

The title of the play, *Much Ado About Nothing*, is a curious one.
We may well ask how the attempted destruction of an innocent
young woman can be described as 'nothing'. Moreover, the
damage is caused by aristocratic men who cannot agree among
themselves, and even Claudio exhibits a callousness that leads
him first to ignore old Leonato and Antonio, and then to joke
with Benedick. Don Pedro does at least say something to the old
men:

> My heart is sorry for your daughter's death:
> But on my honour she was charged with nothing
> But what was true, and very full of proof.
>
> (V. i. 102-4)

'Nothing' but what was true; yet the impact of that nothing on
Hero is appalling.

The motif of woman's faithlessness recurs again in *Troilus and
Cressida* and in *All's Well That Ends Well*; it is also important in
Hamlet, where Gertrude is seen by her son as a symbol of broken
vows and, most obviously, in *Othello* which dates from 1604. For
the plot of *Troilus and Cressida*, Shakespeare returned to classical
legend, and took up the story of the woman who had come to be
the archetypal unfaithful lover to the medieval world. Cressida

swears the vow that the audience, familiar with the story, knows is untrue:

> I know no touch of consanguinity,
> No kin, no love, no blood, no soul so near me
> As the sweet Troilus! O you gods divine,
> Make Cressid's name the very crown of falsehood
> If ever she leave Troilus! Time, force and death,
> Do to this body what extremes you can;
> But the strong base and building of my love
> Is as the very centre of the earth,
> Drawing all things to it.
>
> (IV. ii. 100–8)

But no sooner is she in the Grecian camp, than Ulysses sizes her up and comments that: 'her wanton spirits look out/At every joint and motive of her body' (IV. v. 56–7). Cressida will betray Troilus with very little remorse ('Troilus, farewell! One eye yet looks on thee?/But with my heart the other eye doth see' – V. ii. 106–7) as he watches agonised.

But Cressida's faithlessness is entirely suited to the world of the play, where corruption corrodes the court of Troy and the Greek camp. Hector is murdered by Achilles's men when he is unarmed; the Trojans have clung to ideals of chivalry and love in a world ruled by pragmatic realism. The Greeks will win because they are unscrupulous; they know that Helen is an unfaithful wife, that Agamemnon, as Thersites puts it, 'has not so much brain as ear-wax' (V. i. 51). Helen and Cressida are ruled by sensuality, the Greek warriors are brainless idiots, the Trojans anachronistic idealists. Ulysses, the rationalist, looks dispassionately at both camps and proposes an ideological viewpoint that is profoundly cynical, in which the world can only be stable if force and hierarchy stay in place:

> O, when degree is shaked
> Which is the ladder of all high designs,
> The enterprise is sick. How could communities,
> Degrees in schools, and brotherhoods in cities,
> Peaceful commerce from dividible shores,
> The primogenative and due of birth,

Prerogative of age, crowns, sceptres, laurels,
But by degree stand in authentic place?
Take but degree away, untune that string,
And hark what discord follows.
                                        (I. iii. 101–10)

Tolstoy felt that Shakespeare's handling of the Trojan material demonstrated not only his English chauvinism, but also 'the complete absence of aesthetic feeling in Shakespeare' in comparison with the humanity of Homer.[5] In Shakespeare, he finds:

> a chauvinistic English patriotism, expressed in all the historical dramas, a patriotism according to which the English throne is something sacred, Englishmen always vanquish the French, killing thousands and losing only scores, Joan of Arc is regarded as a witch, and the belief that Hector and all the Trojans, from whom the English descend, are heroes, whilst the Greeks are cowards and traitors and so forth – such is the view of the wisest teacher of life according to his greatest admirers.[6]

Chauvinistic Englishness may be present in Shakespeare, but it would be foolish to take the world of *Troilus and Cressida* at face value, and read it as being only about noble Trojans and ignoble, materialistic Greeks. In this play, as in others from the same period, there is a profound irony in operation. Thersites and Pandarus provide bitter comments on the world, and the last word of the play is left to Pandarus, who concludes with the sour line 'And at that time bequeath you my diseases'. The idealistic values of Troilus and Hector bring about their downfall, but rather than a straight Greek–Trojan dichotomy, what we see is the split between two world-views. The old order is represented by the Trojans, it has no place in the harsh 'real' world of the play; the new order is represented by the Greeks, but as Ulysses reminds us, it will fail unless there is some sense of 'degree', some idea of social structuring that can preserve equilibrium in peace as well as in war. Shakespeare's patriotism was rooted in a sense of the need for stability within the social fabric.

The idea of a sick society is also fundamental to *All's Well That Ends Well*. The settings are all aristocratic – the court of the King of France, the court of the Countess of Roussillon and the court of the Duke of Florence, the only exceptions being the house of the Widow of Florence and the soldiers' camp. All these courts are stricken with some kind of pestilence – the King of France has an apparently incurable malady, the Court of Roussillon has lost the Count and young Bertram cannot succeed his father directly, but must wait for the command of the king to whom he is 'in ward, evermore to subjection' (I. i. 4–5), while the Duke of Florence is at war with the Siennese. The action of the play is set against this background of death, and the opening lines spoken by the widowed Countess remind us that all is set in motion by the loss of her husband: 'In delivering my son from me, I bury a second husband.' The private loss is followed by a second loss, one dictated by the terms of feudal law, under which the son inherits but is bound to the overlord until his majority and then by an oath of fealty, unable to act for himself without his lord's permission.

Against this dark background, the story line follows the fortunes of two figures: Helena and Parolles, who move across class lines in diametrically opposite ways. Helena, described by Coleridge as Shakespeare's 'loveliest character',[7] is in love with Bertram whom she perceives as hopelessly above her socially, and achieves preferment from the king through her magical healing powers. Having cured the incurable, she is then granted the impossible – the right to choose her own husband regardless of his status or inclination. She chooses Bertram, who rejects her and flees from both wife and lord, to the Florentine wars, pausing only before he leaves to issue her with a seemingly hopeless task to fulfil:

> When thou canst get the ring upon my finger, which shall never come off, and show me a child begotten of thy body that I am father to, then call me husband; but in such a 'then' I write a 'never'. (III. ii. 56–60)

Miraculously, just as Helena cures the incurable king, so she succeeds in tricking Bertram to give her both his ring and a child, and after all her trials is restored to the king's protection at the end of the play.

There are no miracles in the Parolles story-line, however,

which charts his fall from a position of arrogance to rejection and degradation where he can state of himself that

> Simply the thing I am
> Shall make me live
> (IV. iii. 338–9)

The insecurity of social status of anyone who is not part of the hereditary aristocracy reveals a society in turmoil, where one turn of the wheel of fortune can make or unmake an individual irrevocably.

Weaving through the rise of Helena and the fall of Parolles is the Florentine–Siennese war. In I. ii when we first meet the king, he is despatching gentlemen to observe 'either part'. Later, in II. i when the gentlemen meet the Duke of Florence, they are at pains not to give a precise opinion as to the rights and wrongs of the conflict, but note that:

> the younger of our nature
> That surfeit on their ease will day by day
> Come here for physic.
> (II. i. 17–19)

And of course this is precisely what Bertram does, when he flees from the French king's court. Arriving in Florence, he is given a command and becomes a military hero. There is therefore a clear contrast between the relationship of fealty to the overlord on the one hand and the idea of foreign wars as places of entertainment and self-trial for bored young aristocrats, deprived of any significant power by their oath of fealty. What emerges from this contrast is a view of two worlds in opposition – the pre-Machiavellian world of the old king and the post-Machiavellian world of young Bertram which recalls the disparity between the world of Trojans and that of the Greeks. The thrust of the play is therefore to show two ideologies in conflict, and the lack of clear-cut resolution at the end only reinforces the sense of crisis and tension within the aristocratic world.

The image of Bertram as military hero, described by the women in III. v, is in contrast to that of the sullen young husband in the earlier part of the play. Readings of Bertram's character

have been greatly influenced by Dr Johnson's famous dismissal
of him as

> A man noble without generosity, and young without truth;
> who marries Helena as a coward and leaves her as a pro-
> fligate: when she is dead by his unkindness, sneaks home to
> a second marriage, is accused by a woman whom he has
> wronged, defends himself by falsehood, and is dismissed to
> happiness.[8]

A major problem for directors of *All's Well That Ends Well* is
indeed presented by the figure of Bertram, for if Dr Johnson's
view is shared, the question must be asked as to what a woman
so virtuous, beautiful and noble-spirited as Helena could ever
find to love in such a man? It would seem that his rashness and
extravagance should be conceived of as 'virtu' in Machiavelli's
sense of the term so that when he appears at the head of
the Florentine army, he comes as the conquering hero, the
Renaissance Prince, a dominant stage figure described by Diana
as a 'most gallant fellow'. In V. iii it is hard not to admire the skill
with which Bertram tries to argue himself out of his increasingly
complicated predicaments, when he lies about the ring, blackens
Diana's name and rejects Parolles, and finally only concedes
defeat when Helena appears, that is, when dealt a blow by
fortune that individual cunning cannot counter. Even at this
stage, however, Bertram is by no means unequivocal. Challenged
directly by Helena with 'Will you be mine now you are doubly
won?', he replies not to her but to the king, in a weak couplet
hinging on a conditional clause:

> If she, my liege, can make me know this clearly
> I'll love her dearly, ever, ever dearly.
>   (V. iii. 314–15)

Helena retorts immediately, in a strong rhyming couplet, with
another conditional, addressed directly to Bertram:

> If it appear not plain and prove untrue
> Deadly divorce step between me and you.
>   (V. iii. 316–17)

It is interesting to note that Helena talks about divorce at this point in the play, the moment when seemingly all wrongs are righted and husband and wife are united at last under the king's protection. It is also somewhat curious, since divorce has been notably absent from the play up to this moment. Bertram, when lamenting his fate to Parolles in II. iii talks about the indissolubility of his marriage – 'Undone and forfeited to cares forever' (II. iii. 263) – and chooses flight from France as his only hope of avoiding a wife he does not want. Helena's reference to 'deadly divorce' in her final lines carries a weight that cannot be overlooked.

Divorce in Reformation England was by no means a clear-cut issue. The Church recognised divorce on grounds of consanguinity of affinity within the prohibited degrees of marriage or for permanent impotence. It also recognised separation *a mensa et thoro*, for cases of adultery or extreme cruelty, but in both categories remarriage was forbidden.[9] In this respect, the Anglican Church differed from most of the other Protestant churches, which allowed remarriage for the innocent party following a divorce, and the divorce debate reached a climax in 1604 (George Hunter dates *All's Well That Ends Well* tentatively as being produced in 1603–4[10]), when No. 107 of the Canons finally forbade the remarriage of divorced persons conclusively.

In her essay on *Arden of Faversham*, Catherine Belsey sums up the political significance of the divorce issue in Elizabethan England:

> The importance of the divorce debate lies in its polarisation of conflicting definitions of marriage. Broadly, the Anglican position was that marriage was indissoluble, that couples were joined by God for the avoidance of fornication and the procreation of children, and that there was no remedy for marital disharmony and discontent. . . . Equally broadly, the Puritans held that marriage was a civil covenant, a thing indifferent to salvation, that it depended on consent, and that where this was lacking the couple could not be said to be joined by God, and could therefore justly be put asunder. . . . The contest for the meaning of marriage cannot be isolated from the political struggles which characterize the century between the Reformation and the English Revolution.[11]

Reading *All's Well That Ends Well* in the light of that divorce debate and the political implications of dissolubility of marriage throws the supposedly fairytale world of the play into different focus. Throughout the play, a major structural feature is the contract-oath, and the binding nature of marriage is explored together with the bond between lord and subject. Both relationships come together in Bertram, the new self-willed aristocrat, recently come into his inheritance but blocked from expressing his will either in public by his overlord, the king. In II. iii, ordered by the king to take Helena as his wife, Bertram accepts in a speech of bitter irony, professing subjection to the king's will while at the same time questioning the basis of the king's power over him:

> Pardon, my gracious lord; for I submit
> My fancy to your eyes. When I consider
> What great creation and what dole of honour
> Flies where you bid it, I find that she, which late
> Was in my nobler thoughts most base, is now
> The praised of the king; who, so ennobled
> Is as 'twere born so.
>
> (II. iii. 167–73)

At this moment of supposedly bowing to the king's wishes, Bertram chooses to talk in terms of his own subjection to the power that the king exercises over him, and, again describing Helena as 'she', refers to the social gulf between them both. She, Helena, being favoured by the king, is as good as ennobled, is the surface message of Bertram's speech, but the deep structure reveals the irony beneath his words. His very acknowledgement of the relationship of fealty between himself and the king is an assertion of his belief in the binding nature of that contract, a contract made by virtue of his aristocratic birth alone, and that belief negates any statement he may make about the ennobling of Helena through actions rather than through blood. Even while appearing to accede to the king's wishes, he is challenging the fundamental premise on which the king's command is being made.

The relationship between king and subject is presented as being based on the subject's acceptance of the king's absolute power, and in the same way the relationship between husband and wife is shown as an indissoluble contract. Bertram enters into two such contracts – publicly, with Helena, and privately, through the exchange of rings with the woman he thinks is Diana. The validity of that private marriage is not called into question – when she sees the ring on Diana's finger, the Countess declares:

> Of six preceding ancestors, that gem
> Conferr'd by testament to th'sequent issue,
> Hath it been owed and worn. This is his wife:
> That ring's a thousand proofs.
>
> (V. iii. 195–8)

The value conferred on the ring by heredity becomes a sign, to the Countess, of Bertram's sincerity, and again the link is made in the text between the inherited power system of the aristocracy and marriage, regardless of whether that marriage has been celebrated before a priest or not. The marriage contract is presented as having an intrinsic value of its own, like the blood relationship of father and son, that cannot be challenged.

It is significant that neither of the marriages are presented on stage. We hear about them both *post facto*, but do not see them take place. Instead, what we do see is the exchange of vows between Helena and the king, when she promises healing and he promises to allow her to choose a husband 'from forth the royal blood of France', and this scene is strongly reminiscent of a marriage. Helena swears an oath that has both a temporal and spatial dimension, showing her total commitment to her task in the following lines:

> If I break time, or flinch in property
> Of what I spoke, unpitied let me die,
> And well deserv'd.
>
> (II. i. 189–91)

This oath is the only one that is actually kept. Bertram allows his private passions to continue to override public declarations of loyalty, hence in his marriage to Helena he has no qualms about declaring his contract before a priest but then refusing to consummate the pact, and likewise, he is willing to consummate but not publicly acknowledge his contract with Diana.

In the decaying courtly world of this play, the whole question of public and private contract is thrown into confusion. What we have is a picture of a society in turmoil, self-destructing, as the old moral idealism of the feudal hierarchy is threatened by the new opportunistic ethos. Bertram struggles to reject feudal authority when it extends into his private life, but fails because his opposition is rooted in an equally hierarchical conception of the world. All he can do is take flight to another court and play at being a military hero. In the end, he is forced to accept the authority of his overlord and publicly acknowledge not only a wife but the heir she presents him with, who offers him the possibility of consolidating his own social position in the future. It is a compromise, but an inevitable one if the courtly class position is to be maintained.

Likewise, Helena's final solution is also a compromise. She has pushed through a contract in spite of the other partner's opposition and in the process has replaced the pre-Reformation idealisation of virginity, with a marriage that ensures her a high social status as she is accepted into the aristocracy. What she does not get is commitment from her partner, and at the end of the play is as far away from a marriage as a union of equal minds as she has ever been. She is bound to Bertram in a power relationship, quite unlike Milton's idealised vision of marriage as 'a covenant, the very being whereof consists not in a forced cohabitation, and counterfeit performance of duties, but in unfeigned love and peace'.[12]

Helena's reference to 'deadly divorce', seen in terms of the interrelatedness of public and private contracts in *All's Well That Ends Well*, and set against the ongoing debate in England about the social basis for divorce is therefore a crucial moment in the play. The Anglican orthodoxy feared divorce as leading to disorder, and as setting a dangerous precedent that might cause other types of contract to be questioned, most particularly that existing between prince and subject. Divorce, in short, was dangerously revolutionary, and it is hardly surprising that Milton should have argued for liberty within marriage as reflecting man's right to liberty within the state:

He who marries intends as little to conspire his own ruin, as he that swears allegiance: and as a whole people is in proportion to an ill government, so is one man to an ill marriage. If they, against any authority, covenant or statute may, my the sovereign edict of charity, save not only their lives but honest liberties from unworthy bondage, as well may he against any private covenant, which he never entered to his mischief, redeem himself from unsupportable disturbances to honest peace and just contentment.[13]

There is a line running through *Much Ado About Nothing*, *Troilus and Cressida* and *All's Well That Ends Well* in which faithfulness and the honouring of a contract between individuals is presented as a metaphoric image of a healthy society. When the pact is broken, the world falls apart. In *Much Ado About Nothing*, that contract is not actually broken, but because Don Pedro and Claudio think it is, the marriage does not take place. In *Troilus and Cressida*, contracts are broken on several levels: Helen has betrayed her husband with Paris, Cressida betrays Troilus with Diomede, Achilles betrays Hector, the ideals of chivalry and 'just war' are themselves betrayed. In *All's Well That Ends Well*, Bertram fails to honour the contract between himself and Helena, and even at the end he has to be coerced into doing so, with the threat of 'deadly divorce' hanging over him.

At a time of crisis, with the passing of the old queen and the accession of a new king, whose position on religion at least was bound to cause further polarisation between monarch and religious groups, with the economy in a precarious state, and hostility from overseas unabated, it is no surprise that Shakespeare should choose to discuss such issues metaphorically from the platform offered him by the theatre. These plays, which look at marriage from a variety of perspectives, also offer a warning to an aristocracy that had grown complacent in its demands for power. Lower-class characters resolve the conflict in *Much Ado About Nothing*; the ignobly born Helena is the character who restores health to the dying court in *All's Well That Ends Well*; the lower-class Pandarus and Thersites comment on the corruption and stupidity of their Greek and Trojan betters. Although these plays may reflect personal bitterness that we can only guess at, it also seems likely that Shakespeare was reminding his audiences of the need for greater openness between partners, whether of different sexes or different classes. The origins of the English revolution, debatable as they have proved to be to historians, nevertheless lie in the turmoil of the later years of Elizabeth's reign and the transition into the Stuart monarchy and in these rather bitter fairytales, we can read signs that the processes of that revolution were already under way.

Notes

Introduction

1. Margot Heinemann, 'How Brecht Read Shakespeare', in Jonathan Dollimore and Alan Sinfield (eds), *Political Shakespeare: New Essays in Cultural Materialism* (Manchester: Manchester University Press, 1985) pp. 202–31.

2. Susan Bassnett, 'Elizabeth Jane Weston: The Hidden Roots of Poetry', in *Prag um 1600* (Luca Verlag: Frankfurt am Main, 1988) pp. 239–5. Susan Bassnett, 'Revising a Biography: A New Interpretation of the Life of Elizabeth Jane Weston, Based on her Autobiographical Poem on the Occasion of the Death of her Mother, *Cahiers Elisabèthains*, no. 37 (April 1990) pp. 1–9.

3. Thomas Babington Macauley, 'Minute on Indian Education', in *Selected Writings*, ed. John Clive and Thomas Pinney (Chicago and London: University of Chicago Press, 1972) pp. 235–53.

4. Leo Tolstoy, 'Shakespeare and the Drama', in Oswald LeWinter (ed.), *Shakespeare in Europe* (Harmondsworth, Middx.: Penguin, 1970) pp. 214–74.

5. Heinrich Heine, 'Shakespeare's Maidens and Women', in LeWinter, *Shakespeare in Europe*, pp. 141–52.

6. Ludwig Tieck, 'Observations Concerning Characters in *Hamlet*', in LeWinter, *Shakespeare in Europe*, pp. 92–111.

7. Grigori Kosintsev, *Shakespeare's Time and Conscience*, trans Joyce Vining (London: Dennis Dobson, 1967) p. 274.

8. Shakespeare provides the basis for vast commercial developments. A huge publishing industry has developed, devoted to discussion of his life and works; countless editions of his plays are still being produced, there are journals dedicated to Shakespeare Studies, huge international conferences, and whole sections of libraries filled with books of criticism. Nor is the industry restricted to publishing: Stratford-upon-Avon has become a place of pilgrimage, an essential

stopover on any tourist's itinerary, and consequently almost every shop in the town is stuffed with commemorative mugs and spoons, Shakespeare trinkets and reproductions of one of the (imaginary) portraits. So great is the power of Shakespeare that in the late 1980s the city of Coventry, home of the University of Warwick, erected new boundary signs stating that Coventry is 'the city in Shakespeare country'. And, of course, as Graham Holderness pointed out in a book that examines what he calls 'the Shakespeare myth', Shakespeare stares out at us from the back of a £20 note (*The Shakespeare Myth* [Manchester: Manchester University Press, 1988]).

9. Jean-Louis Barrault, 'Shakespeare and the French', lecture given during the 1948 Edinburgh Festival, reproduced in LeWinter, *Shakespeare in Europe*, pp. 347–58.

10. George Steevens, Malone, E. *Supplement I*, 654.

11. S. Schoenbaum, *Shakespeare's Lives* (Oxford: Clarendon Press, 1970).

12. M. M. Reese, *Shakespeare: His World and His Work* (London: Edward Arnold, 1980).

13. Ibid., p. 191.

14. T. W. Baldwin, *The Organization and Personnel of the Shakespearean Company* (Princeton, NJ: Princeton University Press, 1927).

15. See Susan Bassnett, 'Struggling with the Past: Women's Theatre in Search of a History', *New Theatre Quarterly*, vol. V, no. 18 (May 1989) pp. 107–13. My suggestion is simply that we need to look again at the kind of evidence collected by Chambers in his study of medieval theatre, for example, where it is quite plain that women were performing with travelling players of all kinds for centuries before the supposed 'arrival of the actress' onto commercial stages. The presence of women in the *commedia dell'arte* companies around Europe shows that England was out of step with other European countries in the late sixteenth century, and what should be explored is the possibility that the absence of women as performers in the licensed companies in England at that time is linked, among other factors, to the new importance of the play and the split between a 'high' text-based theatre on the one hand and on the other, a 'low' theatre (not to be confused with popular theatre in the sense of the term used by Robert Weimann.)

16. Edmund Howes, cited in E. K. Chambers, *The Elizabethan Stage* (Oxford: Oxford University Press, 1923) vol. II, pp. 104–5.

1 Sexuality and Power in the Three Parts of *King Henry VI*

1. Stephen Greenblatt, 'Invisible Bullets', in Jonathan Dollimore and Alan Sinfield (eds), *Political Shakespeare: New Essays in Cultural Materialism* (Manchester: Manchester University Press, 1985) pp. 18–48.

2. Ibid, p. 44.

3. Roy Strong, *Portraits of Queen Elizabeth I* (Oxford: Clarendon Press, 1963). Frances Yates, *Astraea* (London: Routledge, 1975).

4. Quoted in J. E. Neale, *Queen Elizabeth I* (London: Penguin, 1960) p. 302. The authenticity of this speech has been questioned, but even if it transpires that Elizabeth did not address her troops in these terms, there is plenty of documented evidence to show that she often used this kind of imagery.

5. Andrew Cairncross, Introduction to *The Third Part of King Henry VI* (London: Methuen, 1965) p. xlviii.

6. E. Spenser, letter to Sir Walter Raleigh, prefacing *The Faerie Queen* (London: Routledge, 1866) p. x.

2 A Range of Voices: *Titus Andronicus* and *Love's Labour's Lost*

1. Ulrich Bräker, *A Few Words about William Shakespeare's plays by a poor ignorant citizen of the world who had the good fortune to read him*, trans. Derek Bowman (London: Oswald Wolff, 1979) pp. 88–9.

2. Hazlitt, W., *Characters of Shakespeare's Plays* (London: Dent, 1906).

3. S. T. Coleridge, Notes on *Love's Labour's Lost*, *Essays on Shakespeare* (London: Dent, 1907) pp. 71–6.

4 R. W. David, Preface to *Love's Labour's Lost* (London: Methuen, 1951).

5. Muriel Bradbrook, *Shakespeare: The Poet in His World* (London: Methuen, 1978).

6 Peter Thomson, *Shakespeare's Theatre* (London: Routledge and Kegan Paul, 1983) p. 22.

7. Kenneth Muir, *Shakespeare's Tragic Sequence* (London: Hutchinson, 1971) p. 21.

3 The Prison and the World: *Richard III*

1. In her *Shakespeare: the Poet in his World* (London: Methuen, 1978), Muriel Bradbrook suggests that the sequence of writing of a number of poems and plays in the early 1590s can be traced to rivalry between Shakespeare and Marlowe, and certainly the parallels between *Richard II* and *Edward II* are very striking. This rivalry was associated with the two playwrights' relations with the Earl of Southampton, a young nobleman whose friendship with the Earl of Essex and deliberate flouting of the Queen's authority was to lead to his imprisonment for high treason in 1601 and almost to his execution. Shakespeare dedicated his *Venus and Adonis* to Southampton in 1593, and *The Rape of Lucrece* in 1594, and it is possible that Southampton was the mysterious Mr W. H. to whom the Sonnets were later dedicated. Although it is purely speculative, it seems likely that there was a friendship between Shakespeare and Southampton in the early 1590s, and the idea of two talented young writers vying for the patronage and favour of a third man in an environment of intense homoeroticism is an interesting one. Bradbrook points out that we cannot tell the order of the plays, but that

'if *Venus and Adonis* provoked *Hero and Leander*, which in turn led to *Romeo and Juliet*, Shakespeare's *Henry VI* had provoked *Edward II*, to which Shakespeare now replied with *Richard II*'.

2. An interesting insight into the differences of concepts of characterisation can be found by looking at Stanislawski's notes for a production of *Othello* (trans. Helen Novak, *Stanislawski Produces Othello* [London, Geoffrey Bles, 1948]). Stanislawski is at pains to reconstruct character, following his established methodology, but even a cursory reading shows that he has applied twentieth-century criteria and assumes a basis of psychological realism. This causes problems of consistency of characterisation that do not occur at all if we follow Shakespeare's pattern of character shift from scene to scene, as developed through language.

3. Andrew Gurr (ed.), *King Richard II* (Cambridge: Cambridge University Press, 1984).

4. Ibid.

5. Stephen Greenblatt, *The Power of Forms in the English Renaissance* (Norman: Pilgrim Books, 1982).

6. See Jan Kott, *Shakespeare Our Contemporary* (London: Methuen, 1964), and John Elsom (ed.), *Is Shakespeare Still Our Contemporary?* (London: Routledge, 1989).

7. Ulrich Bräker, *A Few Words About William Shakespeare's Plays, by a poor ignorant citizen of the world who had the good fortune to read him*, trans. Derek Bowman (London: Oswald Wolff, 1979) p. 60.

4 Wayward Sons and Daughters: *Romeo and Juliet, A Midsummer Night's Dream* and *Henry IV, Part 1*

1. C. L. Barber, 'The Family in Shakespeare's Development: Tragedy and Sacredness', in Murray M. Schwartz and Coppélia Kahn (eds), *Representing Shakespeare: New Psychoanalytic Essays* (Baltimore and London: The Johns Hopkins Press, 1980) pp. 188–203.

2. Ibid., p. 190.

3. Samuel Pepys, quoted in G. Blakemore Evans, Introduction to the New Cambridge Edition of *Romeo and Juliet* (Cambridge, Cambridge University Press, 1984) p. 33.

4. Bjørnsterne Bjørnson, 'A Defence [of his direction] of *A Midsummer Night's Dream* (1865)', in Oswald LeWinter (ed.), *Shakespeare in Europe* (Harmondsworth, Middx.: Penguin, 1970) pp. 276–84.

5. Jan Kott, *Shakespeare Our Contemporary* (London: Methuen, 1964) p. 81.

6. David Wiles, *Shakespeare's Clown* (Cambridge: Cambridge University Press, 1987).

7. Louis Wright, *Middle-Class Culture in Elizabethan England* (London, Methuen, 1935).

5 The Boundaries of Comedy: *The Taming of the Shrew* and *The Merchant of Venice*

1. See David Wiles, *Shakespeare's Clown* (Cambridge, Cambridge University Press, 1987).
2. Stanley Wells and Gary Taylor (eds), *William Shakespeare: The Complete Works* (Oxford: Clarendon Press, 1986) p. 291.
3. S. T. Coleridge, *Comedy of Errors, Essays and Lectures on Shakespeare and Some Other Old Poets and Dramatists* (London: Dent, 1907) p. 79.
4. Ann Thompson (ed.), *The Taming of the Shrew* (Cambridge, Cambridge University Press, 1984) p. 24.
5 Carol Rutter (ed.), *Clamorous Voices: Shakespeare's Women Today* (London: The Womem's Press, 1988).
6. Lisa Jardine, *Still Harping on Daughters: Women and Drama in the Age of Shakespeare* (Brighton: Harvester Wheatsheaf, 1983) pp. 111 and 113.
7 Louis Wright, *Middle Class Culture in Elizabethan England* (London: Methuen, 1958).
8. Ibid., p. 203.
9. Aristotle, *The Art of Poetry*, in T. S. Dorsch (ed.), *Aristotle, Horace, Longinus: Classical Literary Criticism* (Harmondsworth, Middx.: Penguin, 1965).
10. Thompson, *The Taming of the Shrew*.
11. Trevor Griffiths, *Comedians* (London, Faber and Faber, 1976) p. 20
12. M. M. Mahood (ed.), *The Merchant of Venice* (Cambridge, Cambridge University Press, 1987) p. 48.
13. Ibid., p. 169.
14. José Ortega y Gasset, 'Shylock', in Oswald LeWinter (ed.), *Shakespeare in Europe* (Harmondsworth, Middx.: Penguin, 1963) pp. 329–33.
15. Thomas Moison, '"Which is the merchant here? and which the Jew?": Subversion and Recuperation in *The Merchant of Venice*', in Jean Howard and Marion O'Connor (eds), *Shakespeare Reproduced: The Text in History and Ideology* (London: Methuen, 1987) pp. 188–207.
16. Abraham Hartwell, Dedication to the Archbishop of Canterbury and his translation of Pigafetta, *A Report of the Kingdome of Congo* (1597) quoted in Wright, *Middle Class Culture*, p. 532.
17. Germaine Greer, *Shakespeare* (Oxford: Oxford University Press, 1986) p. 67.

6 England, the World's Best Garden: *Henry IV, Part 2* and *Henry V*

1. P. H. Davison (ed.), *Henry IV, Part II* (Harmondsworth, Middx.: Penguin, 1977).
2. *Stanislawski Produces Othello*, trans. Helen Novak (London: Geoffrey Bles, 1948), p. 163.
3. David Young (ed.), *Twentieth Century Interpretations of Henry IV, Part Two* (Englewood Cliffs, NJ: Prentice-Hall, 1968) p. 1.

4. L. C. Knights, 'Time's Subjects: The Sonnets and *King Henry IV, Part II'*, in *Some Shakespearean Themes* (Stanford, Calif:., Stanford University Press, 1959) reprinted in Young, *Twentieth Century Interpretations of Henry IV, Part Two*, pp. 13–29.

5. Stephen Greenblatt, 'Invisible Bullets: Renaissance Authority and its Subversion, *Henry IV and Henry V'*, in Jonathan Dollimore and Alan Sinfield (eds), *Political Shakespeare: New Essays in Cultural Materialism* (Manchester: Manchester University Press, 1985) p. 44.

6. Andrew Gurr, *Playgoing in Shakespeare's London* (Cambridge: Cambridge University Press, 1987).

7. David Wiles, *Shakespeare's Clown* (Cambridge: Cambridge University Press, 1987).

8. Jonathan Dollimore and Alan Sinfield, 'History and Ideology: The Instance of Henry V', in John Drakakis (ed.), *Alternative Shakespeares* (London: Methuen, 1985) pp. 206–27.

9. Ibid., p. 216.

10. Bertold Brecht, Extract from an introductory talk before his radio version of *Macbeth* on Berlin radio, 14 October 1927, in *Gesammelte werke*, vol. 15, p. 119. Cited in Margot Heinemann, 'How Brecht Read Shakespeare', in Dollimore and Sinfield, *Political Shakespeare*, pp. 202–30.

7 The Play's the Thing: *The Merry Wives of Windsor*

1. Stephen Greenblatt, Invisible Bullets: Renaissance Authority and its Subversion, Henry IV and Henry V', in Jonathan Dollimore and Alan Sinfield (eds), *Political Shakespeare: New Essays in Cultural Materialism* (Manchester: Manchester University Press, 1985) pp. 18–48.

2. See Michel Foucault, *The Order of Things* (London: Tavistock, 1970) esp. ch. 7, also Michel Foucault, *Madness and Civilization* (London: Tavistock, 1967).

3. Andrew Gurr, *The Shakespearean Stage 1574–1642* (Cambridge: Cambridge University Press, 1970) p. 52.

4. Ibid.

5. Ibid, p. 85.

6. M. C. Bradbrook, *Shakespeare: The Poet in his World* (London: Weidenfeld and Nicholson, 1978) p. 140.

7. H. J. Oliver, Introduction to the Arden Edition of *The Merry Wives of Windsor* (London: Methuen, 1971) p. xlv.

8. Ibid, p. xlv.

9. See Gurr, *Shakespearean Stage*.

10 David Wiles, *Shakespeare's Clown* (Cambridge: Cambridge University Press, 1987) p. 133.

11. Ibid., p. 134.

8 Love and Disillusionment: *As You Like It* and *Twelfth Night*

1. See A. C. Swinburne, *Shakespeare* (Oxford: Oxford University

Press, 1909). J. Dover Wilson, *Shakespeare's Happy Comedies* (London: Faber and Faber, 1962).
2. Jan Kott, *Shakespeare Our Contemporary* (London: Methuen, 1964) pp. 69–70.
3. Louis Montrose, '"The Place of a Brother", in *As You Like It*: Social Process and Comic Form', *Shakespeare Quarterly*, vol. 32, no. 1 (Spring 1981) p. 35.
4. Juliet Stevenson, quoted in 'Rosalind, Iconoclast in Arden', in Carol Rutter (ed.), *Clamorous Voices: Shakespeare's Women Today* (London: The Women's Press, 1988) p. 119.
5. Lisa Jardine, *Still Harping on Daughters: Women and Drama in the Age of Shakespeare* (Brighton: Harvester Wheatsheaf, 1983) pp. 20 and 24.
6. Sinead Cusack, quoted in Rutter, *Clamorous Voices*, p. 115.
7. Morton Luce (ed.), Introduction to *Twelfth Night* (London: Methuen, 1906) pp. 8–9.

9 The Rotten State: *Hamlet* and *Julius Caesar*

1. M. C. Bradbrook, *Shakespeare, The Poet in his World* (London: Methuen, 1978) pp. 154–5.
2. Ulrich Bräker, *A Few Words About William Shakespeare's Plays, by a poor ignorant citizen of the world who had the good fortune to read him*, trans. Derek Bowman (London: Oswald Woolf, 1979) p. 99.
3. S. T. Coleridge, *Essays and Lectures on Shakespeare and Some Other Old Poets and Dramatists* (London: Dent, 1907) p. 136.
4. Grigori Kosintzev, *Shakespeare Time and Conscience* (London: Dennis Dobson, 1967) p. 164.
5. David Leverenz, 'The Woman in Hamlet: An Interpersonal View', in Murray M. Schwartz and Coppélia Kahn (eds), *Representing Shakespeare: New Psychoanalytic Essays* (Baltimore and London: The John Hopkins Press, 1980) pp. 110–29, esp p. 123.
6. Wolfgang Clemen, *Shakespeare's Dramatic Art* (London: Methuen, 1972) p. 59.

10 The Fairytale in Crisis: *Much Ado About Nothing, Troilus and Cressida* and *All's Well That Ends Well*

1. Sir John Harington, quoted in J. E. Neale, *Queen Elizabeth I* (Harmondsworth, Middx.: Penguin, 1960) p. 394.
2. Quoted in Peter Thomson, *Shakespeare's Theatre* (London: Routledge, 1983) p. 70.
3. Leonard Digges, quoted in F. H. Mares (ed.), *Much Ado About Nothing* (Cambridge: Cambridge University Press, 1988) p. 10.
4. Jean Howard, 'Renaissance Antitheatricality and the Politics of Gender and Rank in *Much Ado About Nothing*', in Jean Howard and Marion O'Connor (eds), *Shakespeare Reproduced: The Text in History and Ideology* (London: Methuen, 1987) pp. 163–88.
5. Leo Tolstoy, 'Shakespeare and the Drama', in Oswald LeWinter

(ed.), *Shakespeare in Europe* (Harmondsworth, Middx.: Penguin, 1970) p. 254.

6. Ibid., p. 158.

7. S. T. Coleridge, *Essays and Lectures on Shakespeare and Some Other Old Poets and Dramatists* (London: Dent, 1907).

8. Samuel Johnson, *The Plays of William Shakespeare* (London, 1965) vol. III, p. 399.

9. See Lawrence Stone, *The Family, Sex and Marriage in England, 1500–1800* (London: Weidenfeld and Nicolson, 1977) p. 37.

10. See G. K. Hunter (ed.), *All's Well That Ends Well* (London: Methuen, 1967).

11. See Catherine Belsey, 'Alice Arden's Crime', in Catherine Belsey, *The Subject of Tragedy. Identity and Difference in Renaissance Drama* (London: Methuen, 1985) pp. 129–49.

12. John Milton, 'The Doctrine and Disciplines of Divorce', in K. M. Burton (ed.), *Milton's Prose Writings* (London: Dent, 1958) pp. 247–319, see esp. p. 261.

13. Ibid., pp. 251–2.

Bibliography

The vast number of works on Shakespeare that continue to appear annually make the task of compiling a succinct bibliography almost impossible. The titles of books listed below include those that the present writer has found useful and thought provoking. The list contains classic works on Shakespeare, together with more recent material and further, more detailed bibliographies can be found in many of the volumes cited.

Editions and Series
William Shakespeare, *The Complete Works*, ed. Peter Alexander (London, 1951).
William Shakespeare, *The Complete Works*, general ed. Alfred Harbage (Baltimore and London, 1969).
William Shakespeare, *The Complete Works*, general eds Stanley Wells and Gary Taylor (Oxford, 1986).

New Arden Shakespeare, ed. Una Ellis Fermor, Harold F. Brookes and Harold Jenkins (London: Methuen, 1951–).
New Cambridge Shakespeare, ed. Philip Brockbank (Cambridge: Cambridge University Press, 1984–).
New Penguin Shakespeare, ed. T. J. B. Spenser and Stanley Wells (Harmondsworth, Middx.: Penguin, 1967–).
New Variorum Shakespeare, ed. H. H. Furness (Philadelphia, 1971–).
Oxford Shakespeare, ed. Stanley Wells and Gary Taylor (Oxford: Oxford University Press, new spelling edn, 1986– ; old spelling edn, 1987–).

C. L. Barber, *Shakespeare's Festive Comedy* (Princeton, NJ: Princeton University Press, 1959).
John Barton, *Playing Shakespeare* (London: Methuen, 1984).

Catherine Belsey, *The Subject of Tragedy: Identity and Difference in Renaissance Drama* (London: Methuen, 1985).

M. C. Bradbrook, *Shakespeare: The Poet in his World* (London: Weidenfeld and Nicolson, 1978).

Ulrich Bräker, *A Few Words about William Shakespeare's Plays by a poor ignorant citizen of the world who had the good fortune to read him* (London: Oswald Woolf, 1979).

Anthony Brennan, *Onstage and Offstage Worlds in Shakespeare's Plays* (London: Routledge, 1989).

Philip Brockbank (ed.), *Players of Shakespeare* (Cambridge: Cambridge University Press, 1985).

John Russell Brown, *Shakespeare and his Comedies* (London: Methuen, 1957).

——, *Shakespeare's Plays in Performance* (London, 1966).

Dympna Callaghan, *Women and Gender in Renaissance Tragedy* (London, 1989).

E. K. Chambers, *The Elizabethan Stage*, 4 vols (Oxford: Oxford University Press, 1923).

——, *William Shakespeare*, 2 vols (Oxford: Oxford University Press, 1930).

Wolfgang Clemen, *Shakespeare's Dramatic Art* (London: Methuen, 1972).

Jonathon Dollimore, *Radical Tragedy: Religion, Ideology and Power in the Drama of Shakespeare and his Contemporaries* (Brighton, 1985; 2nd edn, 1989).

—— and Alan Sinfield (eds), *Political Shakespeare: New Essays in Cultural Materialism* (Manchester: Manchester University Press, 1985).

John Drakakis, *Alternative Shakespeares* (London: Methuen, 1985).

—— (ed.), *Shakespearean Tragedy* (London, 1991).

Terry Eagleton, *William Shakespeare* (Oxford: Basil Blackwell, 1986).

John Elsom (ed.), *Is Shakespeare Still Our Contemporary?* (London: Routledge, 1989).

Hugh Grady, *The Modernist Shakespeare: Critical Texts in a Material World* (Oxford, 1991).

Stephen Greenblatt, *Renaissance Self-fashioning: From More to Shakespeare* (Chicago: University of Chicago, 1980).

—— (ed.), *The Forms of Power and the Power of Forms in the Renaissance* (Norman: University of Oklahoma, 1982).

——, *Shakespearian Negotiations: The Circulation of Social Energy in Renaissance England* (Oxford, 1988).

—— (ed.), *Representing the English Renaissance* (Los Angeles and London, 1988).

——, *Learning to Curse: Essays in Early Modern Culture* (London, 1990).

Germaine Greer, *Shakespeare* (Oxford: Oxford University Press, 1986).

Andrew Gurr, *The Shakespearean Stage 1574–1642* (Cambridge: Cambridge University Press, 1970).

Terence Hawkes, *Shakespeare's Talking Animals* (London: Edward Arnold, 1973).

——, *That Shakespearean Rag: Essays on a Critical Process* (London: Methuen, 1986).

Terence Hawkes, *Meaning by Shakespeare* (London, 1992).

Graham Holderness, *The Shakespeare Myth* (Manchester: Manchester University Press, 1988).

Jean Howard and Marion O'Connor (eds), *Shakespeare Reproduced: The Text in History and Ideology* (London: Methuen, 1987).

Jan Kott, *Shakespeare Our Contemporary* (London: Methuen, 1964).

Lisa Jardine, *Still Harping on Daughters: Women and Drama in the Age of Shakespeare* (London: Harvester, 1988).

Grigori Kozintsev, *Shakespeare, Time and Conscience* (London: Dennis Dobson, 1967).

Kathleen McCluskie, *Renaissance Dramatists* (London, 1989).

Philip McGuire, *Speechless Dialect: Shakespeare's Open Silences* (Berkeley, Calif.: University of California Pres, 1985)

—— and D. Samuelson (eds), *Shakespeare: The Theatrical Dimension* (New York: AMS Press, 1979).

C. W. R. D. Moseley, *Shakespeare's History Plays* (Harmondsworth, Middx.: Penguin, 1988).

Kenneth Muir, *Shakespeare's Tragic Sequence* (London: Hutchinson, 1972).

——, *The Sources of Shakespeare's Plays* (London: Methuen, 1977).

Stephen Mullaney, *The Place of the Stage: License, Play, and Power in Renaissance England* (Chicago and London, 1988).

Patricia Parker and Geoffrey Hartmann (eds), *Shakespeare and the Question of Theory* (London: Methuen, 1985).

M. M. Reese, *Shakespeare: His World and his Work* (Cambridge: Cambridge University Press).

Anne Righter, *Shakespeare and the Idea of the Play* (Cambridge: Cambridge University Press, 1962).

Carol Rutter (ed.), *Clamorous Voices: Shakespeare's Women Today* (London: The Women's Press, 1988).

S. Schoenbaum, *Shakespeare: A Documentary Life* (Oxford: Oxford University Press, 1975).

J. L. Styan, *Shakespeare's Stagecraft* (Cambridge: Cambridge University Press, 1967).

Leonard Tennenhouse, *Power on Display: The Politics of Shakespeare's Genres* (London: Methuen, 1986).

Peter Thompson, *Shakespeare's Theatre* (London: Routledge and Kegan Paul, 1983).

E. M. W. Tillyard, *The Elizabethan World Picture* (London, 1943).

H. Aram Veser (ed.), *The New Historicism* (New York and London, 1989).

Robert Weimann, *Shakespeare and the Popular Tradition in the Theatre: Studies in the Social Dimension of Dramatic Form and Functions*, ed. Robert Schwantz (Baltimore: The Johns Hopkins University Press, 1978).

Robin Headlam Wells, *Shakespeare, Politics and the State* (London: Macmillan, 1986).

Stanley Wells (ed.), *Shakespeare: Select Bibliographica; Guides* (Oxford, 1990).

David Wiles, *Shakespeare's Clown: Actor and Text in the Elizabethan Playhouse* (Cambridge: Cambridge University Press, 1987).

Index